Carpet Python.

Carpet Pythons As Pets.

Carpet Python daily care, pro's and cons, cages, costs, diet, biology and health.

By

Ben Team

ALL RIGHTS RESERVED. This book contains material protected under International and Federal Copyright Laws and Treaties.

Any unauthorized reprint or use of this material is strictly prohibited. No part of this book may be reproduced or transmitted in any form or by any means, electronic, mechanical or otherwise, including photocopying or recording, or by any information storage and retrieval system without express written permission from the author.

Copyrighted © 2016

Published by: IMB Publishing

Table of Contents

Table of Contents 3

About the Author 5

Foreword 6

PART I: THE CARPET PYTHON 8

Chapter 1: Physical Description and Anatomy 9

Chapter 2: Biology and Behavior 16

Chapter 3: Classification and Taxonomy 21

Chapter 4: The Carpet python's World 24

PART II: CARPET PYTHON HUSBANDRY 27

Chapter 5: Carpet Pythons as Pets 28

Chapter 6: Providing the Captive Habitat 42

Chapter 7: Establishing the Thermal Environment 47

Chapter 8: Lighting the Enclosure 60

Chapter 9: Substrate and Furniture 63

Chapter 10: Maintaining the Captive Habitat 73

Chapter 11: Feeding Carpet Pythons 80

Chapter 12: Water and Humidity 85

Chapter 13: Interacting with Your Carpet Python 90

Chapter 14: Common Health Concerns 96

Chapter 15: Breeding Carpet pythons 106

Chapter 16: Further Reading 116

References 121

Index 123

About the Author

Ben Team is an environmental educator and author with over 16 years of professional reptile-keeping experience.

Ben currently maintains www.FootstepsInTheForest.com, where he shares information, narration and observations of the natural world. When not writing about plants, animals and habitats, Ben enjoys spending time with his beautiful wife.

Foreword

Carpet pythons are medium-sized, gloriously patterned animals native to Australia and the island of Papua.

They exhibit rather typical biology and behavior for a python, as they are primarily nocturnal animals who subsist on rodents, birds and lizards, which they subdue via constriction.

It is only when the fine details are considered that they become so obviously well suited for captivity.

At the outset, one must appreciate the hardy nature of carpet pythons. In their natural homelands, carpet pythons are "weedy" species, which often occur at relatively high densities and survive amid the human-wildland boundaries.

Many are encountered in suburban and urban locations, and unlike many other species, which have very specific habitat requirements, such as the closely related black pythons (*Morelia boeleni*) that only survive in the highland forests of New Guinea, carpet pythons are adaptable snakes that can survive in a variety of different microhabitats.

This combination of their adaptability and hardy constitutions help carpet pythons adjust well to captive life. As evidence of this fact, consider that the vast majority of carpet pythons in European and North American collections are the product of several generations of captive breeding efforts.

However, this adaptability is not the only thing that makes carpet pythons excellent pets. After all, corn snakes (*Pantherophis guttatus*), royal pythons (*Python regius*) and many other snakes are similarly well adapted for captive maintenance. But for the snake enthusiast who likes something a little bigger, carpet pythons fit the bill.

In fact, carpet pythons are the ideal size for many snake keepers. Carpet python size varies with species, subspecies and sex, but most carpet pythons fall somewhere in the 5- to 6-foot range. This is arguably the ideal size for someone who wants a "large" – rather than "giant" -- snake. However, discretion is necessary when picking a pet carpet python, as the females of some populations may approach 10 feet or so in length, which, by most measures, is a bit too large for casual snake keepers.

Carpet pythons are also arboreal or semi-arboreal snakes that are often inclined to spend a large portion of their lives perching on their cage branches, which makes them phenomenal display animals.

Many other snakes live arboreal lives, but few of these species tolerate handling as well as carpet pythons do. While carpet pythons often enter the world feeling defensive, and are quick to bite that fingers that hold them, most become tractable, tame animals over time.

However, even those few carpet pythons that never tame down continue to be wonderful pets – most carpet pythons display very attractive colors and markings, and some are among the most beautifully marked snakes in the world.

Spectacular examples of jungle carpet pythons (*Morelia spilota cheynei*), for example, are clad in breathtaking black-and-gold colors that must be seen in person to fully appreciate. Additionally, with the development of several color mutations, prospective keepers have a variety of aesthetics from which they can choose.

Snake selection always requires careful thought and planning, but for those interested in pets that offer a relatively unique combination of size, markings, temperament and habits, carpet pythons are hard to beat.

PART I: THE CARPET PYTHON

Properly caring for any animal requires an understanding of both the species and its place in the natural world. This includes subjects as disparate as anatomy and ecology, diet and geography, and reproduction and physiology.

It is only by learning what your pet is, how it lives and what it does, that you can achieve the primary goal of animal husbandry: Providing your pet with the highest quality of life possible.

Chapter 1: Physical Description and Anatomy

Thanks in part to their striking markings, carpet pythons (*Morelia spilota* ssp.) are relatively easy to recognize. However, their similarities to not begin and end here -- several other traits characterize this group of snakes. For example, like most other arboreal and semi-arboreal species, carpet pythons have relatively slender builds and long, prehensile tails.

Size

Hatchlings carpet pythons generally emerge from their eggs measuring about 15 to 19 inches (0.3 to 0.5 meters) in length, and weighing a little less than 1 ounce (20 to 30 grams). By the time they have reached maturity, most adults measure between 5 and 7 feet (1.5 and 2.1 meters).

There is, however, great variation in the average adult size of the different subspecies. The smallest forms – jungle (*Morelia spilota cheynei*) and Irian Jaya carpet pythons (*Morelia spilota "harrisoni"*) – typically range between 4 and 6 feet in length, while the largest forms – coastal carpet pythons (*Morelia spilota mcdowelli*) occasionally reach 10 to 12 feet (3 to 4 meters) in length.

Females grow larger than males do in some populations, but males grow larger in others. (D. Person, 2002) (S. Fearn, 2002) (Fitzgerald R. S., 1995) Additionally, the degree of sexual dimorphism varies from one locality to the next. (D. Person, 2002) Many western carpet python populations, for example, exhibit greater dimorphism than eastern populations do. Some western carpet python populations include females that are twice the size of the mature males. (D. Pearson, 2002)

Scalation

The scalation of carpet pythons varies from one subspecies to the next, as well as among individuals of a given subspecies. Although there a few generalized trends are present there is great overlap among the species; accordingly, scale counts are poor criteria for identifying subspecies.

Most carpet pythons bear 40 to 60 scale rows at mid-body. Their dorsal and lateral scales are small, and essentially diamond-shaped, while their ventral scales, which usually number between 239 and 300, are wide and plate-like. Their anal plate is undivided, yet most of their subcaudal scales (which typically number between 63 and 91) are paired.

Most carpet python head scales are small and granular, but the prefrontal and internasal scales are typically large and plate-like. Additionally, some carpet pythons possess a large scale in the frontal region.

Many of the upper and lower labial scales of carpet pythons bear sensory pits, which allow the snakes to detect thermal information about their environment. (Proske, 1968)

Color and Pattern

Few snakes are as variably colored and patterned as carpet pythons are. Most bear the same basic markings, but variations exist among the various subspecies and populations, as well as among individuals of a given clutch.

The striking markings of carpet pythons contribute significantly to their popularity.

In general, carpet pythons are chiefly clad in three different colors, but some individuals feature four, five or six colors.

The darkest color usually dominates, with lighter bands, blotches, stripes or spots overlaying the ground color. Many carpet pythons also exhibit light colors between the light-colored bands.

The ground color varies from black in jungle carpet pythons and diamond pythons, to light brown, gray or tan in Irian Jaya and coastal carpet pythons.

Hatchlings of most species appear different from their parents; most carpet pythons undergo a rather significant color change as they age. Many hatchling carpet pythons display some red coloration, but this usually disappears by the time they reach adulthood.

Eyes and Ears

Carpet pythons see movement well, but their visual acuity is limited. However, their limited vision works well in both light and dark conditions.

Snakes lack moveable eyelids, meaning that their eyes are open at all times – even while they sleep. In fact, it can be difficult (if not impossible) to tell whether a motionless snake is sleeping or awake. To protect their eyes, snakes have a clear scale covering each eye, called the spectacle. Like all other scales on the snake's body, they shed their spectacles periodically.

Carpet pythons have variably colored irises and elliptical pupils that resemble those of a cat. While frequently presumed to be a trait associated with nocturnal activity patterns, research indicates that such eyes are more likely an adaptation to ambush – rather than prowling – hunting styles. (F. BRISCHOUX, 2010)

Like all other snakes, carpet pythons lack external ears entirely and only possess rudimentary inner ears. Although scientists debate the precise extent to which snakes can hear airborne sounds (if at all), it is clear that they do not hear airborne sounds well.

Nevertheless, snakes readily detect vibrations through direct contact with the substrate, which allows them to detect the footsteps of approaching predators.

The Tongue, Nose and Vomeronasal Organ

The forked tongue of snakes is one of their most famous characteristics. As with other snakes, carpet pythons use their tongues solely for sensory purposes – they play no role in feeding or sound production. Most carpet pythons have dark-colored tongues.

The tongue extends from the mouth to collect volatile particles from the environment. Then, when the tongue is withdrawn, it transfers these particles to the vomeronasal organ. The vomeronasal organ provides the snakes with an additional chemical sense, somewhat akin to smell or taste.

Snakes use their nostrils – located at the front of the face -- to detect airborne chemicals in the environment, and they have a very strong sense of smell. The vomeronasal organ (located in the roof of the mouth), has two openings – one for each tip of the snake's tongue. This allows snakes to process directional information picked up by the tongue.

Mouth and Teeth

Carpet pythons have a mouth full of sharp, recurved teeth, primarily designed for catching and holding prey.

The teeth are attached rather weekly to the surface of the jawbones. Like all other snakes, carpet pythons continually lose and replace teeth throughout their lives. Sometimes keepers will find shed teeth in their snake's cage or contained within its feces.

Like most other pythons, carpet pythons bear teeth on all five of the tooth bearing bones found in snakes: the maxillary, palatine, pterygoid, premaxillary and dentary bones. However, when looking into the mouth of a living specimen, you will see four different rows of teeth.

The dentary bones produce a half-circle of teeth along the edge of the bottom jaw, while the maxillaries produce a similar half-circle of teeth along the edge of the top jaw. The pterygoid and palatine bones (four bones in total) anchor two roughly straight rows of teeth that lie longitudinally along the roof of the snake's mouth. The premaxillary teeth lie at the very front of the mouth along the top jaw.

Thermal Receptivity

Carpet pythons have numerous indentations in some of their labial scales. These "pits" attach to thermally sensitive nerves, which carry thermal information to the brain.

In the brain, this thermal information is thought to be superimposed over visual information. The result is that carpet pythons are likely able to "see" thermal information about their environment.

This helps the snakes in myriad ways. The difference in temperature between a warm-blooded bird or rodent and the cool night air makes such prey conspicuous, regardless of their cryptic coloration or morphology. Similarly, the snakes can better see warm-blooded predators at a distance, and act accordingly.

It is also possible that carpet pythons and similarly equipped snakes use the information derived from this thermal imaging system to aid their thermoregulatory behavior.

The Tail and Vent

Carpet pythons have relatively long, prehensile tails, which help them to grip branches while climbing. Because males carry their hemipenes inside their tail bases, they have proportionately longer and thicker tails (and therefore a greater number of subcaudal scales) than females do.

A small opening – called the vent – is located on the ventral surface of the tail base. The vent leads directly to the cloaca, and serves as the final exit point for waste, urates and eggs.

When snakes defecate, release urates or copulate, the vent opens slightly.

Internal Organs

Snakes have internal organs that largely mirror those of other vertebrates, except that snakes tend to stagger their paired organs, such as kidneys, testis and ovaries.

The digestive system begins with the esophagus, which accepts food from the mouth and transports it to the stomach. A long intestinal tract transports food from the stomach to the anus where the food residue is expelled. Along the way, the liver, gall bladder, spleen and pancreas aid the digestive process by producing and storing digestive enzymes.

Snakes propel blood through their bodies via a heart and circulatory system. Unlike advanced snakes (such as rat snakes, kingsnakes, vipers and elapids), which only have a single functional lung, carpet pythons are very primitive snakes that possess two lungs.

Like most other animals, snakes filter their blood and manage their water levels with their kidneys. Snakes produce uric acid as a byproduct of protein synthesis, and expel it through the vent. This uric acid often looks like pieces of chalk, and is not soluble in water.

The nervous system of carpet pythons is comprised of a relatively small brain and nerve fibers, which extend through the rest of the snake's body. The nervous system provides them with information about the outside world and controls their body movements.

One interesting anatomical feature of carpet pythons (as well as all other snakes) is their flexible windpipe. Known as the glottis, the tube transports air to and from the lungs and resides in the bottom of snakes' mouths. Snakes have the ability to move their glottis in order to breathe while they are swallowing large food items.

Skeletal System

Snakes have elongated bodies, so they have many more vertebrae than most other vertebrates do. Each vertebrae attaches to two of the python's rib bones (typically, snakes have one vertebrae for every ventral scale and subcaudal pair). The degree of flexibility between each vertebra is much greater in carpet pythons and other constricting snakes, than it is in species that do not constrict their prey.

As demonstrated by their skeletal systems, carpet pythons are very primitive snakes. Unlike advanced snakes that hail from more recent lineages, pythons have retained the pelvic girdle of their lizard ancestors. However, like all living snakes, carpet pythons show no trace of shoulder girdles. Extending from the pelvic girdle are two rudimentary leg bones. Horny caps cover the end of these bones and penetrate through the body wall, extending outside of the snake's body. Snake keepers often refer to these appendages as "spurs."

Carpet pythons have conscious control their spurs, but they do not use them for locomotion. Males use their spurs to stimulate females during courting. Very large individuals can have massive spurs, which can cause serious scratches if such snakes are handled carelessly. Males generally have larger spurs than females do, but this is not a reliable method for determining sex. In addition to individual variability, spurs can break and wear down over time.

Reproductive Organs

Male carpet pythons have paired reproductive structures that they hold inside their tail base. The males evert these organs, termed hemipenes (singular: hemipenis), during mating activities and insert them inside the females' cloacas.

Females also have paired reproductive systems, which essentially mirror those of other vertebrates. One key difference is the presence of structures called oviducts. Oviducts hold the male's sperm and accept the ova after they are released from the ovaries during ovulation.

Chapter 2: Biology and Behavior

Carpet pythons have evolved a number of biological and behavioral adaptations that allow them to survive in their natural habitats. While they share some of these adaptations with their close relatives, others are unique to carpet pythons.

Locomotion

Carpet pythons may employ several different methods of locomotion, but they primarily crawl via a method called rectilinear motion. When climbing, carpet pythons primarily use a method called concertina motion.

Carpet pythons do not hold a monopoly on these methods – both rectilinear and concertina motion are common locomotor methods for many large-bodied snakes, including other pythons, pythons and vipers.

Rectilinear motion occurs when the carpet pythons use a section of their ventral and lateral muscles to swing their ventral scales forward, grip the substrate, and then pull the snake forward. The process allows the snakes to crawl forward in a straight line.

Concertina motion involves extending the head and neck in the direction of an accessible perch. The head and chin then grip and pull against the perch, which brings the snake's rear body forward.

Like most snakes, carpet pythons are capable swimmers.

Shedding

Like other animals, snakes must shed their outer skin layers as they wear out. While mammals do so continuously, snakes shed their entire external layer of skin cells at periodic intervals.

This process may occur as frequently as once every month when snakes are young and growing quickly, or as rarely as two or three times per year for larger, mature snakes.

Snakes that are injured, ill or parasitized may shed more frequently than usual. Some shedding events, such as the snake's first shed, or the females' post-ovulation shed, mark important milestones.

The shedding process takes approximately 7 to 10 days to complete. Initially, the snake begins producing a layer of fluid between the two outermost layers of skin. This serves as a lubricant that helps the old skin to peel off.

After a day or two, this fluid may become visible and give the snakes a cloudy appearance. It is often most apparent when viewing the snake's ventral surface or eyes. Because clear scales cover the eyes of snakes, the fluid makes the eyes of most pre-shed snakes look very cloudy and blue. At this time, the snake's vision is impaired, and most snakes spend this time hiding.

A few days later, the snake's eyes clear up, and it looks normal again. A day or two later, the snake will begin the process of shedding.

Snakes begin the process by trying to cut the old layer of skin on their lips. They do this by rubbing their faces against stationary surfaces. While many keepers incorporate rough surfaces in the cage for fear that the snake will not be able to shed without them, this is rarely a problem in practice. The cage walls are usually more than adequate for the purpose.

After separating the skin on the lips, the old skin starts to peel away. The snake crawls forward, leaving the old skin behind. The fresh, clean new skin usually looks much brighter than it did just a few days earlier.

Metabolism and Digestion

Carpet pythons are ectothermic ("cold-blooded") animals, whose internal metabolism depends on their internal body temperature. When carpet pythons are warm, their bodily functions proceed more rapidly; when they are cold, their bodily functions proceed slowly.

This also means that carpet pythons digest more effectively at suitably warm temperatures than they do at suboptimal temperatures. Their appetites also vary with temperature, and if the temperatures drop below the preferred range, they may cease feeding entirely.

A carpet python's body temperature largely follows ambient air temperatures, but they also absorb and reflect radiant heat, such as that coming from the sun. They adjust their behavior as necessary to keep their internal temperatures within their preferred range.

In general, pythons prefer lower body temperatures and have slower metabolic rates than most similarly sized reptiles. (Christian, 1998)

Growth Rate and Lifespan

Carpet pythons exhibit a growth rate that is similar for most other medium-sized pythons. Most reach 3-feet (1 meter) in length by their first birthday, and the majority have reached maturity by their third or fourth birthday.

Carpet pythons are long-lived animals, who routinely live for 10 to 15 years in captivity. Their maximum lifespan is unknown, but reliable records exist for animals that are approximately 20 years of age.

Their lifespan is likely shorter in the wild, without the benefit of veterinary care and unlimited food.

Foraging Behavior

Carpet pythons occasionally prowl for food, but they are primarily ambush predators. Carpet pythons may adopt ambush postures in trees of varying heights or on the ground. (Fitzgerald R. S., 1996) Often, carpet pythons select ambush locations that are in close proximity to a desirable prey source. (G. W. Heard, 2004)

Adults may forage or lie in ambush at any time of the day or night, but they are typically more active at night. Some evidence suggests that juveniles – particularly those living in areas with cool night temperatures – may not be able to remain active for long after the sun sets. Whereas adults are able to remain within the preferred temperature range for up to 8 hours after basking in the afternoon, small animals cool to the ambient temperatures within 1 to 2 hours. (Shine, 1997)

Many carpet pythons have been observed setting up in ambush postures in fruit trees, presumably to capture small birds and mammals that feed on the fruit.

Defensive Strategies and Tactics

The primary way by which carpet pythons avoid predators is a combination of their reclusive nature and cryptic coloration. Additionally, they tend to be most active during periods of low light.

However, this habit of avoiding detection is not infallible, and a combination of avian and mammalian predators locate these snakes from time to time. When this happens, carpet pythons may unleash a litany of defensive behaviors.

Hissing is one of the most common defensive tactics in which carpet pythons engage. If this fails to deter the attacker, they will typically resort to biting, but they may also defecate, exude foul smelling musk from the vent or constrict the would-be predator.

Reproduction

Much of what is known about carpet python reproduction has been derived from captive breeding efforts. Although each subspecies exhibits variations on the theme, most carpet pythons breed in the spring, and deposit eggs in the late spring or early summer.

Like most other female pythons, carpet python females coil around their egg clutch, guarding it and incubating it for the rest of the developmental process. The young hatch from mid- to late-summer.

Some male carpet pythons may exhibit agonistic behavior toward other males, while others may remain peaceful when they encounter other males. Females do not engage in combat with other females.

Females probably only produce eggs every other year, although those who can secure enough food may produce clutches in successive years.

Chapter 3: Classification and Taxonomy

Understanding the way scientists classify carpet pythons provides valuable insight for those who keep them as pets.

The common name "carpet python" is applied to several different subspecies of snakes. The group's organization has been the subject of great debate – dozens of authors have embraced an equally diverse number of arrangements.

Further exacerbating this problem is the lack of studies examining the entire group – most have restricted their analysis to only a portion of the whole group.

A formal investigation of the group's composition is beyond the scope of this work, and of little interest to the typical snake enthusiast. Accordingly, the arrangement listed below has been selected because it is widely used by snake keepers, and is therefore most relevant to the reader.

For more information about the taxonomy of the group, refer to (Lyons, 2011), (O'Shea, 2007), (O'Shea, 1996) and (Barker, 1994).

The basic classification of carpet pythons is as follows:

Kingdom: Animalia

Phylum: Chordata

Class: Reptilia

Order: Squamata

Family: Boidae

Subfamily: Pythoninae

Genus: *Morelia*

Species: *spilota*

Subspecies: *cheynei, mcdowelli, variegata, imbricata, metcalfei* and *"harrisoni"*

The nominate subspecies – the diamond python (*Morelia spilota spilota*) – is not commonly considered a carpet python. This is due to a combination of factors, including the color patterns of diamond pythons, which differ markedly from all other *Morelia spilota* subspecies; the geographic range of the animals, which extends farther from the equator than any other python; and the corresponding differences in behavior and biology, which developed in response to (or in concert with) their geographic range.

Morelia spilota spilota – Diamond python

Morelia spilota cheynei – Jungle carpet python

Morelia spilota "harrisoni" / variegata – Irian Jaya carpet python

Morelia spilota imbricata – Southwestern carpet python

Morelia spilota mcdowelli – Coastal carpet python

Morelia spilota metcalfei – Inland carpet python

Morelia spilota variegata– Northwest carpet python

The Irian Jaya carpet python is recognized as a distinct form by many authors (some of whom use the subspecies name *harrisoni*), but others consider it part of the northwest carpet python subspecies (*Morelia spilota variegata*). (O'Shea, 1996)

The jungle carpet python, Irian Jaya carpet python and coastal carpet python are undoubtedly the most common forms seen in North American and European collections.

As explained earlier, most carpet python subspecies exhibit great visual variation, so it is often difficult to distinguish one form from another for novices. Aside from the diamond python, all other forms of the species thrive under relatively similar maintenance regimes, so this is of little concern for the average hobbyist.

Two other members of the *Morelia* genus – the Bredl's python (*Morelia bredli*) and the rough scaled python (*Morelia carinata*) – bear a superficial resemblance to carpet pythons, but belong to different species.

Diamond pythons look quite different from their carpet python relatives.

Chapter 4: The Carpet python's World

To maintain a carpet python successfully, you must understand the animal's native habitat so that you can provide a reasonable facsimile of it.

Range

Carpet pythons are native to parts of Australia and the island of New Guinea. Each of the different subspecies inhabits a slightly different range, although intermediate-looking specimens often occur along shared boundaries.

- Diamond pythons inhabit parts of New South Wales and the extreme eastern portions of Victoria.
- Coastal carpet pythons are found along most of the eastern Australia, from Queensland and the northern tip of New South Wales.
- The inland carpet python's range lies to the west of the coastal and diamond pythons, including parts of Queensland, New South Wales, Victoria and South Australia.
- The northwestern carpet python is found across the northern portion of the continent, including parts of Queensland, the Northern Territory and Western Australia.
- Southwestern carpet pythons are restricted to the southwestern portion of Western Australia.
- Jungle carpet pythons inhabit a small region in eastern Queensland.
- The Irian Jaya carpet python occurs along the southern portions of New Guinea.

Climate

Carpet pythons experience a wide variety of climates across their range. Those in New Guinea and northern Australia experience a tropical climate, characterized by warm temperatures throughout the year and seasonal rains.

By contrast, carpet pythons living in the southern portions of Australia experience a temperate climate, with warm summers and cool winters.

As a general rule, the climate of the Australian Interior is arid, while New Guinea and northern Queensland receive ample rainfall each year.

Habitat

Carpet pythons are habitat generalists, which can thrive in most non-desert habitats. Forests and densely vegetated thickets are preferred by most subspecies, although Irian Jaya carpet pythons inhabit relatively open-canopied tropical forests near the coast, and eschew rainforest habitats. (Lyons, 2011)

Carpet pythons are frequently found inhabiting suburban areas, and they turn up in backyards, university campuses, agricultural regions and city parks with regularity.

Some inland carpet python populations are known to shift from one habitat to another during the year. After spending the winter in rocky areas and transitioning through wooded habitats during the spring, they move into open areas with abundant secondary growth during the summer. They reverse the cycle in the second half of the year. (G. W. Heard, 2004)

Natural Diets

Carpet pythons are opportunistic feeders, who have been recorded consuming a wide variety of prey species. Hatchlings and juveniles primarily consume lizards, whereas adults shift to a bird- and mammal-dominated diet.

In addition to native mammals and birds, carpet pythons also consume feral and introduced species, such as European rabbits (*Oryctolagus cuniculus*). (G. W. Heard, 2004)

Carpet pythons have been documented consuming household pets on numerous occasions, including pet birds and housecats.

Natural Predators

Hatchling and juvenile carpet pythons must avoid a wide variety of predators, including other snakes, large lizards, birds of prey and mammalian carnivores.

The primary predators for adult carpet pythons are wild dogs and foxes. (Heard, et al., 2006) However, large birds of prey and goannas occasionally consume carpet pythons as well.

Vehicular traffic and intolerant humans also kill a significant number of adult carpet pythons.

PART II: CARPET PYTHON HUSBANDRY

Once equipped with a basic understanding of what carpet pythons *are* (Chapter 1 and Chapter 3), where they *live* (Chapter 4), and what they *do* (Chapter 2) you can begin learning about their captive care.

Animal husbandry is an evolving pursuit. Keepers shift their strategies frequently as they incorporate new information and ideas into their husbandry paradigms.

There are few "right" or "wrong" answers, and what works in one situation may not work in another. Accordingly, you may find that different authorities present different, and sometimes conflicting, information regarding the care of carpet pythons.

In all cases, you must strive to learn as much as you can about your pet and its natural habitat, so that you may provide it with the best quality of life possible.

Chapter 5: Carpet Pythons as Pets

Carpet pythons can make rewarding pets, but you must know what to expect before adding one to your family. This includes not only understanding the nature of the care they require, but also the costs associated with this care.

Assuming that you feel confident in your ability to care for a carpet python and endure the associated financial burdens, you can begin seeking your individual pet.

Understanding the Commitment

Keeping a carpet python as a pet requires a substantial commitment. You will be responsible for your pet's well-being for the rest of its life. This is an especially important consideration, given that carpet pythons are rather long-lived animals.

Can you be sure that you will still want to care for your pet a decade or more into the future? Do you know what your living situation will be? What changes will have occurred in your family? How will your working life have changed over this time?

You must consider all of these possibilities before acquiring a new pet. Failing to do so often leads to apathy, neglect and even resentment, which is not good for you or your snake.

Neglecting your pet is wrong, and in some locations, a criminal offense. You must continue to provide quality care for your carpet python, even once the novelty has worn off, and it is no longer fun to clean the cage and feed him each week.

Once you purchase a carpet python, its well-being becomes your responsibility until it passes away at the end of a long life, or you have found someone who will agree to adopt the animal for you.

Unfortunately, this is rarely an easy task. You may begin with thoughts of selling your pet to help recoup a small part of your investment, but these efforts will largely fall flat.

While professional breeders may profit from the sale of carpet pythons, amateurs are at a decided disadvantage. Only a tiny sliver of the general population is interested in reptilian pets, and only a small subset of these are interested in keeping carpet pythons.

Of those who are interested in acquiring a carpet python, most would rather start fresh, by purchasing a small hatchling or juvenile from an established breeder, rather than adopting your questionable animal for free.

After having difficulty finding a willing party to purchase or adopt your animal, many owners try to donate their pet to a local zoo. Unfortunately, this rarely works either.

Zoos are not interested in your pet python, no matter how pretty and tame he is. He is a pet with little to no reliable provenance and questionable health status. This is simply not the type of animal zoos are eager to add to their multi-million dollar collections.

Zoos obtain most of their animals from other zoos and museums; failing that, they obtain their animals directly from their land of origin. As a rule, they do not accept donated pets.

No matter how difficult it becomes to find a new home for your unwanted python, you must never release non-native reptiles into the wild.

Carpet pythons may be able to colonize places outside their native range, and released or escaped reptiles cause distress to those who are frightened by them. This leads municipalities to adopt pet restrictions or ban reptile keeping entirely.

The Costs of Captivity

Reptiles are often marketed as low-cost pets. While true in a relative sense (the costs associated with dog, cat, horse or tropical fish husbandry are often much higher than they are for carpet pythons), potential keepers must still prepare for the financial implications of carpet python ownership.

At the outset, you must budget for the acquisition of your pet, as well as the costs of purchasing or constructing a habitat. Unfortunately, while many keepers plan for these costs, they typically fail to consider the on-going costs, which will quickly eclipse the initial startup costs.

Startup Costs

One surprising fact most new keepers learn is the enclosure and equipment will often cost as much or more than the animal does (except in the case of very high-priced specimens).

Prices fluctuate from one market to the next, but in general, the least you will spend on a carpet python is about $75 (£50), while the least you will spend on the *initial* habitat and assorted equipment will also be about $100 (£70). Replacement equipment and food will represent additional (and ongoing) expenses.

Young carpet pythons are often defensive.

Examine the charts on the following pages to get an idea of three different pricing scenarios. While the specific prices listed will vary based on innumerable factors, the charts are instructive for first-time buyers.

The first scenario details a budget-minded keeper, trying to spend as little as possible. The second example provides a cost estimate for a keeper with a moderate budget, and the third example provides a case study for extravagant shoppers, who want an expensive carpet python and top-notch equipment.

These charts are only provided as estimates; your experience may vary based on a variety of factors.

Inexpensive Option	
Neonate Coastal Carpet Python	$75 (£50)
Small Plastic Storage Box	$10 (£7)
Screen and Hardware for Lid	$10 (£7)
Heat Lamp Shroud and Bulb	$20 (£14)
Digital Indoor-Outdoor Thermometer	$15 (£10)
Infrared Thermometer	$35 (£24)
Economy Water Dish	$5 (£3)
Economy Hide	$5 (£3)
Forceps, Spray Bottles, Misc. Supplies	$20 (£14)
Total	$195 (£135)

Moderate Option	
Hatchling Jungle Carpet Python	$150 (£105)
Economy Plastic Cage	$100 (£70)
Economy Radiant Heat Panel	$20 (£14)
Economy Thermostat	$50 (£35)
Digital Indoor-Outdoor Thermometer	$15 (£10)
Infrared Thermometer	$35 (£24)
Economy Water Dish	$5 (£3)
Two Economy Hides	$10 (£7)
Forceps, Spray Bottles, Misc. Supplies	$20 (£14)
Total	$405 (£280)

Premium Option	
Albino Carpet Python	$1000 (£700)
Premium Plastic Cage	$250 (£175)
Premium Radiant Heat Panel	$100 (£70)
Premium Thermostat	$150 (£105)
Digital Indoor-Outdoor Thermometer	$15 (£10)
Infrared Thermometer	$35 (£25)
Premium Water Dish	$15 (£10)
Two Premium Hides	$30 (£21)
Forceps, Spray Bottles, Misc. Supplies	$20 (£14)
Total	$1615 (£1130)

Ongoing Costs

The ongoing costs of carpet python ownership primarily fall into one of three categories: food, maintenance and veterinary care.

Food costs are the most significant of the three, but they are relatively consistent and somewhat predictable. Some maintenance costs are easy to calculate, but things like equipment malfunctions are impossible to predict with any certainty. Veterinary expenses are also hard to predict, and they vary wildly from one year to the next.

Food Costs

Food is the single greatest ongoing cost you will experience while caring for your carpet python. To obtain a reasonable estimate of your yearly food costs, you must consider the number of meals you will feed your snake per year and the cost of each meal.

Most carpet pythons will consume between 25 and 50 food items per year. Hatchlings will eat "hopper" or small adult mice; large adults require medium or large rats.

The cost of feeder rodents varies drastically depending upon the source. It is much cheaper to purchase them in bulk, but you must allow for shipping costs when purchasing bulk rodents. Retail rodents typically cost about three times the price of those purchased in bulk.

For example, bulk hopper mice may cost $0.35 (£0.25) or so each, while single hopper mouse in a pet store is likely to cost $1.00 (£0.72) or more. Likewise, a small rat is about $1.00 (£0.72) when purchased in bulk, but will cost you at least $3.00 (£2.16) to purchase from a pet store.

Extrapolated over the course of a year, these differences become significant. For example, if may cost you about $17.50 (£12.57) to purchase 50 hoppers mice in bulk, or $50 (£35) to purchase them from your local pet shop. As long as the shipping costs are less than

$32.50 (£23.35), it makes more sense to purchase the animals in bulk.

Veterinary Costs

While experienced keepers may be able to avoid going to the vet for regular examinations, novices should visit their veterinarian at least once every year.

Assuming your snake is healthy, you may only need to pay for an office visit. However, if your vet sees signs of illness, you may find yourself paying for cultures, medications or procedures. Wise keepers budget at least $200 to $300 (£144 to £215) for veterinary costs each year.

Maintenance Costs

It is important to plan for both routine and unexpected maintenance costs.

Commonly used items, such as paper towels, disinfectant and substrate are rather easy to calculate. However, it is not easy to know how many burned out light bulbs, cracked misting units or faulty thermostats you will have to replace in a given year.

Those who keep their carpet pythons in simple enclosures will find that about $50 (£35) covers their yearly maintenance costs. By contrast, those who maintain elaborate habitats may spend $200 (£144) or more each year.

Myths and Misunderstandings

Snakes are the subject for countless myths and misunderstandings. It is important to rectify any flawed perceptions you may have, before welcoming one into your life.

Myth: Snakes grow in proportion to the size of their cage and then stop.

Fact: Snakes do no such thing. Healthy snakes grow throughout their lives, although the rate of growth slows with age. Placing them in a small cage in an attempt to stunt their growth is an unthinkably cruel practice, which is more likely to sicken or kill the snake than stunt its growth.

Myth: Snakes can sense fear.

Fact: Snakes are not magical creatures. They are constrained by physics and biology just as humans, dogs and squid are. With that said, it is possible for some animals to read human body language very well. Some long-time keepers have noticed differences in the behavior of some snakes when people of varying comfort levels handle them. This difference in behavior may be confused with the snake "sensing fear."

Myth: Snakes must eat live food.

Fact: While snakes primarily hunt live prey in the wild, a few species consume carrion when the opportunity presents itself. In captivity, most snakes learn to accept dead prey. Whenever possible, hobbyists should feed dead prey to their snakes to minimize the suffering of the prey animal and reduce the chances that the snake will become injured.

Myth: Snakes have no emotions and do not suffer.

Fact: While snakes have very primitive brains, and do not have emotions comparable to those of higher mammals, they can absolutely suffer. Always treat snakes with the same compassion you would offer a dog, cat or horse.

Myth: Snakes prefer elaborately decorated cages that resemble their natural habitat.

Fact: While some snakes thrive better in complex habitats that offer a variety of hiding and thermoregulatory options, they do not appreciate your aesthetic efforts.

Unlike humans, who experience the world through their eyes, snakes experience the world largely as they perceive it through their vomeronasal system. Your carpet python is not impressed with the rainforest wallpaper decorating the walls of his cage.

Additionally, while many snakes require hiding spaces, they do not seem to mind whether this hiding space is in the form of a rock, a rotten log or a paper plate. As long as the hiding spot is safe and snug, they will utilize it.

Myth: Carpet pythons automatically constrict any animal with which they come into contact.

Fact: Carpet pythons are very strong constrictors, but they do not engage in constricting behavior unless they are trying to subdue prey or, rarely, when defending themselves from predators. When held, carpet pythons often hang on tightly, but this is of little concern. Nevertheless, it is a bad idea to allow any constricting snake to wrap around your neck.

Acquiring Your Carpet Python

Modern reptile enthusiasts can acquire carpet pythons from a variety of sources, each with a different set of pros and cons.

Pet stores are one of the first places many people see carpet pythons, and they become the de facto source of pets for many beginning keepers. While they do offer some unique benefits to prospective keepers, pet stores are not always the best place to purchase carpet pythons; so, consider all of the available options, including breeders and reptile swap meets, before making a purchase.

Pet Stores
Pet stores offer a number of benefits to keepers shopping for carpet pythons, including convenience: They usually stock all of the equipment your new snake needs, including cages, heating devices and food items.

Additionally, they offer you the chance to inspect the snake up close before purchase. In some cases, you may be able to choose from more than one specimen. Many pet stores provide health guarantees for a short period, which provide some recourse, should your new pet fall ill.

However, pet stores are not the ideal place to purchase your new pet. Pet stores are retail establishments, and as such, you will usually pay more for your new pet than you would from a breeder.

Additionally, pet stores rarely know the pedigree of the animals they sell, and they will rarely know the snake's date of birth, or other pertinent information. Only a handful of pet stores will be able to distinguish among the various carpet python species, so specimens may also be mislabeled.

Other drawbacks associated with pet stores primarily relate to staff inexperience. While some pet stores concentrate on reptiles and may educate their staff about proper carpet python care, others fail to do so, leading their employees to provide incorrect advice to customers.

It is also worth considering the increased exposure to pathogens that pet store animals endure, given the constant flow of animals through such facilities.

Reptile Expos
Reptile expos offer another option for purchasing a carpet python. Reptile expos often feature resellers, breeders and retailers in the same room, all selling various types of carpet pythons and other reptiles.

Often, the prices at such events are quite reasonable and you are often able to select from many different snakes. However, if you have a problem with the snake later on, it may be difficult to find the seller once the event has concluded.

Breeders
Because they usually offer unparalleled information and support to their customers, breeders are generally the best place for most novices to shop for carpet pythons. Additionally, breeders often know the species well, and are better able to help you learn the husbandry techniques necessary for success.

For those seeking rare or unusual carpet pythons, breeders are often the only option. The same principle holds true for those seeking spectacular individuals from proven bloodlines – the only place to purchase such carpet pythons are from breeders.

The primary disadvantage of buying from a breeder is that you must often make such purchases from a distance, either by phone or via the internet. Nevertheless, most established breeders are happy to provide you with photographs of the animal you will be purchasing, as well as his or her parents.

Selecting Your Carpet Python
There are three primary considerations to make when selecting a carpet python: sex, age and personality.

The Sex
Aside from breeding attempts, the husbandry of carpet pythons is essentially identical for both sexes. Some keepers assert that females eat more aggressively than males do, but this has yet to be proven empirically.

Nevertheless, females are usually in higher demand by breeders, so males are often less expensive than females are. One exception to this rule occurs when new color or pattern mutations appear on the market. In such circumstances, males are often more expensive than females are.

The Age
Novices can be successful with neonatal carpet pythons, but slightly older specimens, who have already become established and have started feeding regularly, are preferred.

Because they may have become accustomed to their long-term homes, mature specimens are not good selections for novices.

Ideally, beginners should purchase yearlings, as they are more forgiving of errors than young animals are.

The Personality
Advanced hobbyists and breeders may consider a snake's personality to be a low priority in comparison to its species, gender, age and other factors. However, for new keepers, personality can be an important criterion.

When purchasing yearlings or older snakes, beginners can try to select calm individuals (as long as they eat readily). However, when selecting a neonate, it often behooves the keeper to select an aggressive – but not nervous – animal, as aggressive animals are often easier to feed.

Health Checklist

Always check carpet pythons thoroughly for signs of injury or illness before making the purchase. If you are purchasing the animal from someone in a different part of the country, you must inspect it immediately upon delivery. Notify the seller promptly if the animal exhibits any health problems.

Avoid the temptation to acquire or accept a sick or injured animal in hopes of nursing him back to health. Not only are you likely to incur substantial veterinary costs while treating your new pet, you will likely fail in your attempts to restore the snake to full health. Sick carpet pythons rarely recover in the hands of novices.

Additionally, by purchasing injured or diseased animals, you incentivize poor husbandry on the part of the retailer. If retailers lose money on sick or injured animals, they will take steps to avoid this eventuality. They may do this by acquiring healthier stock in the first place, or by providing better care for their charges – either way improves the lives of the snakes in their care.

As much as is possible, inspect the following features:

- **Observe the snake's skin**. It should be free of lacerations and other damage. Pay special attention to those areas that frequently sustain damage, such as the tail tip, vent and snout. A small cut or abrasion may be relatively easy to treat, but significant abrasions and cuts may become infected and often require significant treatment.

- **Gently check the snake for mites and ticks**. Mites are about the size of a flake of pepper, and they may be black, brown or red. Mites often move about on the snake, whereas ticks – if attached and feeding – do not move. Avoid purchasing animals with either parasite. Additionally, you should avoid purchasing any other animals from this source, as they are likely to harbor parasites as well.

- **Examine the snake's eyes and nostrils**. The eyes should look turgid and clear (unless the snake is entering a shed cycle), and they should be free of discharge. The nostrils should be clear and dry – snakes with runny noses or those who blow bubbles are likely to be suffering from a respiratory infection.

- **Gently palpate the animal and ensure no lumps or anomalies are apparent**. Lumps in the muscles or abdominal cavity may indicate parasites, abscesses or tumors.

- **Check the snake's vent**. The vent should be clean and free of smeared feces. Smeared feces can indicate parasites or bacterial infections.

Quarantine

Because new animals may have illnesses or parasites that could infect the rest of your collection, it is wise to quarantine all new acquisitions. This means that you should keep any new animal as far away from the rest of your snake collection as possible. Only once you have ensured that the new animal is healthy should you introduce it to the main colony.

During the quarantine period, you should keep the new snake in a simplified habitat, with a paper substrate, water bowl, basking spot and a few hiding places. Keep the temperature and humidity at ideal levels.

It is wise to obtain fecal samples from your snake during the quarantine period. You can take these samples to your veterinarian, who can check them for signs of internal parasites. Always treat any existing parasite infestations before removing the animal from quarantine.

Always tend to quarantined animals last, as this reduces the chances of transmitting pathogens to your healthy animals. Do not wash quarantined water bowls or cage furniture with those belonging to your healthy animals. Always be sure to wash your hands thoroughly after handling quarantined animals, their cages or their tools.

Quarantine new acquisitions for a minimum of 30 days; 60 or 90 days is even better.

Chapter 6: Providing the Captive Habitat

In most respects, providing carpet pythons with a suitable captive habitat requires that you functionally replicate the various aspects of their wild habitats.

Providing your carpet python with appropriate housing is the most important aspect of captive care. In essence, the habitat you provide to your pet becomes his world.

Remember: There are few absolutes regarding reptile husbandry. What works for most keepers and snakes may not work for you and your pet. Additionally, advanced keepers are often able to sidestep problems that trouble beginners.

Habitat Dimensions and Layout

Throughout their lives, snakes need a cage large enough to lay comfortably, access a range of temperatures and get enough room for exercise.

The rule of thumb for most snakes is to ensure that the animal is no longer than ½ the length of the cage's perimeter.

Generally speaking, this means that hatchlings and young snakes require about 1 to 2 square feet of space (0.10 to 0.20 square meters). Large, mature animals require about 6 to 8 square feet (0.5 to 0.75 square meters) of space.

Carpet pythons climb frequently in the wild, so cages with a bit of height are preferred. However, this is not to suggest that they need vertically oriented cages – the longest dimension of the cage should extend from side to side, not top to bottom. Most cages used for hatchlings and juveniles offer plenty of cage height, while adults will best thrive in cages with 18 to 24 inches (45 to 60 centimeters) of height. Providing more height than this may make it difficult to heat the habitat appropriated.

In addition to total space, the layout of the cage is also important – rectangular cages are strongly preferable to square, round or octagonal cages for a variety of reasons:

- They allow the keeper to establish better thermal gradients.
- Cages with one long direction allow your snake to stretch out better than a square cages do.
- If the cage is accessible via front-opening doors, you will not have to reach as far back in a rectangular cage as you would a square cage when cleaning.

Enclosure Types

In the "old days," those inclined to keep reptiles had few choices with regard to caging. The two primary options were to build a custom cage from scratch or construct a lid to use with a fish aquarium.

By contrast, modern hobbyists have a variety of options from which to choose. Review each style carefully before making your decision – each style provides its own set of advantages and disadvantages.

Aquariums

Aquariums are popular choices for snake cages, largely because of their ubiquity. Virtually any pet store that carries snakes also stocks aquariums.

Aquariums can make suitable snake cages, but they have a number of drawbacks.

- Aquariums (and other glass cages) are hard to clean
- Aquariums are very fragile
- Aquariums do not retain heat very well
- Aquariums require an after-market or custom built lid
- Aquariums often develop water spots from repeated mistings

When aquariums are used with screened tops, the excess ventilation may cause the tank to dry out rapidly. This can be a challenge for carpet python keepers in dry areas, as they attempt to keep their snake's habitat suitably humid. To work around this, some keepers attach plastic or glass covers over a portion of the screened lid.

Commercial Cages

Commercially produced cages have a number of benefits over other enclosures. Commercial cages usually feature doors on the front of the cage, which provide better access than top-opening cages do. Additionally, bypass glass doors or framed, hinged doors are generally more secure than after-market screened lids are.

Plastic cages are usually produced in dimensions that make more sense for snakes, and often have features that aid in heating and lighting the cage.

Commercial cages can be made out of wood, metal, glass or other substances, but the majority are made from PVC or ABS plastic.

Commercial cages are available in two primary varieties: those that are molded from one piece of plastic and those that are assembled from several different sheets. Assembled cages are less expensive and easier to construct, but molded cages have few (if any) seams or cracks in which bacteria and fungus can thrive.

Some cage manufacturers produce cages in multiple colors. White is probably the best color for novices, as it is easy to see dirt, mites and other small problems. A single mite crawling on a white cage surface is very visible, even from a distance.

Black cages do not show dirt as well. Such cages are most appropriate for more experienced keepers who have developed proper hygiene techniques over time. Additionally, carpet pythons are beautiful when viewed against black cage walls.

While carpet pythons have cone cells in their retinas, and *may* be able to see color, it is unlikely that cage color is a significant factor in their quality of life. If you worry about this, it is probably best to choose a dark or earth-toned color.

Plastic Storage Containers

Plastic storage containers, such as those used for shoes, sweaters or food, make suitable cages for small carpet pythons. However, the lids for plastic storage boxes are rarely secure enough for use with snakes.

Hobbyists and breeders overcome this by incorporating Velcro straps, hardware latches or other strategies into plastic storage container cages.

The best way to use plastic storage containers is with a wooden or plastic rack. Such systems are often designed to use containers without lids. In these "lidless" systems, the shelves of the rack form the top to the cage sitting below them. The gap between the top of the sides of the storage containers and the bottom of the shelves is usually very tight – approximately one-eighth inch (2 millimeters) or less.

When plastic containers are used, you must drill or melt numerous holes for air exchange. If you are using a lid, it is acceptable to place the holes in the lid; however, if you are using a lidless system, you will have to make the holes in the sides of the boxes.

Drill or melt all of the holes from the inside of the box, towards the outside of the box. This will help reduce the chances of leaving sharp edges inside the cage, which could cut the snake.

If you intend to heat a single plastic storage box with a heat lamp, you will need to cut a hole in the lid, and cover the hole with hardware cloth or screen. Attach the mesh or hardware cloth with silicone or cable ties. You can now place the heat lamp on top of the mesh.

Homemade Cages

For keepers with access to the necessary tools and materials (as well as the desire and skill to use them), it is possible to construct homemade cages.

A number of materials are suitable for cage construction, and each has different pros and cons. Wood is commonly used, but must be adequately sealed to avoid rotting, warping or absorbing offensive odors.

Plastic sheeting is a very good material, but few have the necessary skills, knowledge and tools necessary for cage construction. Additionally, some plastics may have extended off-gassing times.

Glass can be used, whether glued to itself or when used with a frame. Custom-built glass cages can be better than aquariums, as you can design them in dimensions that are appropriate for snakes. Additionally, they can be constructed in such a way that the door is on the front of the cage, rather than the top.

Regardless of the materials used, security and safety are of paramount importance when constructing a custom cage.

Screen Cages

Screen cages make excellent habitats for some lizards and frogs, but they are not suitable for carpet pythons. Screened cages do not retain heat well, and they are hard to keep suitably humid.

Additionally, screen cages are difficult to clean and often develop weak spots that can give the inhabitant enough of a hole to push through and escape.

This jungle carpet python displays the "zebra" mutations.

Chapter 7: Establishing the Thermal Environment

Providing the proper thermal environment is one of the most important aspects of reptile husbandry. As ectothermic ("cold blooded") animals, carpet pythons rely on the local temperatures to regulate the rate at which their metabolism operates.

Snakes deprived of access to suitable temperatures spend a great deal of time at the veterinarian's office, battling infections and illness. Accordingly, you must provide your python with an appropriate thermal environment.

This requires you to understand the temperature range appropriate for carpet pythons, the correct techniques for achieving such temperatures, and the equipment needed to do so.

Thermometers

It is important to monitor the cage temperatures very carefully to ensure your pet stays health. Just as a water test kit is an aquarist's best friend, quality thermometers are some of the most important husbandry tools for reptile keepers.

Two different types of temperature are relevant for pet snakes: **ambient temperatures** and **surface temperatures**.

The ambient temperature in your animal's enclosure is the air temperature; the surface temperatures are the temperatures of the objects in the cage. Both are important to monitor, as they can differ widely.

For example, the air temperatures may be 90 degrees Fahrenheit (32 degrees Celsius) outside on a hot summer day, but the surface of a black rock may be in excess of 120 degrees Fahrenheit (49 degrees Celsius).

The differences between ambient and surface temperatures can significantly affect your snake's health. For example, surface temperatures of 120 degrees Fahrenheit (49 degrees Celsius) may burn your animal, but they may not kill your pet. Conversely, ambient temperatures in this range will quickly prove fatal.

Measure the cage's ambient temperatures with a digital thermometer. An indoor-outdoor model will feature a probe that allows you to measure the temperature at both ends of the thermal gradient at once. For example, you may position the thermometer at the cool side of the cage, but attach the remote probe to a branch near the basking spot.

Because standard digital thermometers do not measure surface temperatures well, use a non-contact, infrared thermometer for such measurements. These devices will allow you to measure surface temperatures accurately from a short distance away.

The Preferred Temperature Range of Carpet Pythons

Ambient temperatures of about 86 degrees Fahrenheit (30 degrees Celsius) are close to ideal for carpet pythons. They become more susceptible to illness if exposed to temperatures below about 65 degrees Fahrenheit (18 degrees Celsius), and they may begin to demonstrate signs of stress at ambient temperatures exceeding 90 degrees Fahrenheit (32 degrees Celsius).

Wild carpet pythons living in areas with cold winters experience temperatures lower than 65 degrees Fahrenheit (18 degrees Celsius), and some breeders subject their animals to similar temperatures for breeding purposes. However, it is generally unwise for beginners to expose their snakes to such low temperatures.

Thermal Gradients

In their natural habitat, carpet pythons can keep their bodies within these preferred ranges by altering their behavior. For example, a wild carpet python who is trying to digest a large meal may bask on a sunny branch. The same python may retreat into a rodent burrow later that day, to avoid the oppressive heat.

You want to provide similar opportunities for your captive python by creating a thermal gradient. The best way to do this is by clustering the heating devices at one end of the habitat, which creates a basking spot (the warmest spot in the enclosure).

Because no heating devices are placed at the opposite end of the cage, the temperature will slowly drop with increasing distance from the basking spot. This arrangement creates a *gradient* of temperatures.

By establishing a gradient in the enclosure, your captive carpet python will be able to access a range of different temperatures. This will allow him to manage his body temperature just as his wild counterparts do.

Adjust the heating device until the surface temperature at the basking spot is about 90 to 95 degrees Fahrenheit (32 to 35 degrees Celsius). Ambient temperatures at the basking spot should be in the high 80s Fahrenheit (30 to 31 degrees Celsius). Provide a slightly cooler basking spot for small individuals, with maximum surface temperatures of about 88 degrees Fahrenheit (31 degrees Celsius).

Ideally, the cool end of the cage should be in the low 70s Fahrenheit (22 to 23 degrees Celsius) during the day, when the heat source is on.

This range of temperatures will allow your snake to maintain his body temperature at the preferred level, somewhere in the middle of this range.

The need to establish a thermal gradient is one of the most compelling reasons to use a large cage. In general, the larger the cage, the easier it is to establish a suitable thermal gradient.

Heating Equipment

A variety of heating devices are available to carpet python keepers. Each has its own set of pros and cons, so wise keepers consider the decision carefully before deciding which type of heat source to use.

Heat Lamps

Heat lamps are one of the best choices for supplying heat to carpet pythons. Heat lamps consist of a reflector dome and an incandescent bulb. The light bulb produces heat (in addition to light) and the metal reflector dome directs the heat to a spot inside the cage.

If you use a cage with a metal screen lid, you can rest the reflector dome directly on the screen; otherwise, you will need to clamp the lamp to something over the cage. Always be sure that the lamp will not be dislodged by vibration, children or pets.

In the interest of fire safety, it is wise to opt for heavy-duty reflector domes with ceramic bases, rather than economy units with plastic bases.

While you can use specialized light bulbs that are designed for use with reptiles, they are not necessary. Regular, economy, incandescent bulbs work well. Snakes do not require special lighting, and incandescent bulbs – even those produced for use with reptiles – rarely generate much UVA, and never generate UVB.

One of the greatest benefits of using heat lamps to maintain the temperature of your snake's habitat is the inherent (and affordable) flexibility with these types of heating devices.

Heat lamps offer flexibility in two ways:

- **Changing the Bulb Wattage**

The simplest way to adjust the temperature of your python's cage is by changing the wattage of the bulb being used. For example, if a 40-watt light bulb is not raising the temperature of the basking spot high enough, you may try a 60-watt bulb. Alternatively, if a 100-

watt light bulb is elevating the cage temperatures higher than are appropriate, switching the bulb to a 60-watt model may help.

- **Adjusting the Height of the Heat Lamp**

The closer the heat lamp is to the cage, the warmer the cage will be. Use this characteristic to your advantage. For example, if the habitat is too warm, the light can be raised, which should lower the cage temperatures slightly.

However, the higher the heat lamp is raised, the larger the basking spot becomes. Accordingly, it is important to be careful that you do not raise the light too high, which results in reducing the effectiveness of the cage's thermal gradient. In very large cages, this may not compromise the thermal gradient very much, but in a small cage, it may eliminate the "cool side" of the habitat entirely.

In other words, if your heat lamp creates a basking spot that is roughly 1-foot in diameter when it rests directly on the screen, it may produce a slightly cooler, but larger basking spot when raised 6-inches above the level of the screen.

Ceramic Heat Emitters
Ceramic heat emitters are small inserts that function similarly to light bulbs, except that they do not produce any visible light – they only produce infrared radiation (heat).

Ceramic heat emitters are used in reflector-dome fixtures, just as heat lamps are. The benefits of such devices are numerous:

- They typically last much longer than light bulbs do
- They are suitable for use with thermostats
- They allow for the creation of overhead basking spots, as lights do
- They can be used day or night

However, the devices do have three primary drawbacks:

- They are very hot when in operation
- They are much more expensive than light bulbs

- You cannot tell by looking if they are hot or cool. This can be a safety hazard – touching a ceramic heat emitter while it is hot is likely to cause serious burns.

Radiant Heat Panels

Quality radiant heat panels are the best choice for heating most reptile habitats, including those containing carpet pythons.

Radiant heat panels are essentially heat pads that are attached to the roof of the habitat. They usually feature plastic or metal casings and internal reflectors to direct the heat back into the cage.

Radiant heat panels have a number of benefits over traditional heat lamps and under tank heat pads:

- They do not contact the animal at all, thus reducing the risk of burns.
- They do not produce visible light, which means they are useful for both diurnal and nocturnal heat production. They can be used in conjunction with fluorescent light fixtures during the day, and remain on at night once the lights go off.
- They are inherently flexible. Unlike many devices that do not work well with pulse-proportional thermostats, most radiant heat panels work well with on-off and pulse-proportional thermostats.

The only real drawback to radiant heat panels is their cost: radiant heat panels often cost about two to three times the price of light- or heat pad-oriented systems. However, many radiant heat panels outlast light bulbs and heat pads, a fact that offsets their high initial cost over the long term.

Heat Pads

Heat pads are an attractive option for many new keepers, but they are not without drawbacks.

- Heat pads can cause contact burns.
- If they malfunction, they can damage the cage as well as the surface on which they are placed.

- They are more likely to cause a fire than heat lamps or radiant heat panels are.

However, if installed properly (which includes allowing fresh air to flow over the exposed side of the heat pad) and used in conjunction with a thermostat, they can be reasonably safe. With heat pads, it behooves the keeper to purchase premium products, despite the small increase in price.

Heat Tape

Heat tape is somewhat akin to a "stripped down" heat pad. In fact, most heat pads are simply pieces of heat tape that have already been connected and sealed inside a plastic envelope.

Heat tape is primarily used to heat large numbers of cages simultaneously. It is generally inappropriate for novices, and requires the keeper to make electrical connections. Additionally, a thermostat is always required when using heat tape.

Historically, heat tape was used to keep water pipes from freezing – not to heat reptile cages. While some commercial heat tapes have been designed specifically for reptiles, many have not. Accordingly, it may be illegal, not to mention dangerous, to use heat tapes that are not specifically designed for reptile-related applications.

Heat Cables

Heat cables are similar to heat tape, in that they heat a long strip of the cage, but they are much more flexible and easy to use. Many heat cables are suitable to use inside the cage, while others are designed for use outside the habitat.

Always be sure to purchase heat cables that are designed specifically for reptile cages. Those sold at hardware stores are not appropriate for use in snake cages.

Heat cables must be used in conjunction with a thermostat, or, at the very least, a rheostat.

Heated, Faux Rocks

In the early days of commercial reptile products, faux rocks, branches and caves with internal heating elements were very popular. However, they have generally fallen out of favor among modern keepers. These rocks and branches were often made with poor craftsmanship and cheap materials, causing them to fail and produce tragic results. Additionally, many keepers used the rocks improperly, leading to injuries, illnesses and death for many unfortunate reptiles.

Heated rocks are not designed to heat an entire cage; they are designed to provide a localized source of heat for the reptile. Nevertheless, many keepers tried to use them as the primary heat source for the cage, resulting in dangerously cool cage temperatures.

When snakes must rely on small, localized heat sources placed in otherwise chilly cages, they often hug these heat sources for extended periods of time. This can lead to serious thermal burns – whether or not the units function properly. This illustrates the key reason why these devices make adequate supplemental heat sources, but they should not be used as primary heating sources.

Modern hot rocks utilize better features, materials and craftsmanship than the old models did, but they still offer few benefits to the keeper or the kept. Additionally, any heating devices that are designed to be used inside the cage necessitate passing an electric cable through a hole, which is not always easy to accomplish. However, some cages do feature passageways for chords.

Room Heat

Some keepers with very large collections elect to heat the entire room, rather than individual cages. While this is an economic and viable solution for advanced keepers, it is not appropriate for novices.

Heating the whole room, instead of an individual cage, makes it very difficult to achieve a good thermal gradient. Experienced keepers may be able to maintain their snakes successfully in this manner, but beginners should always rely on the added safety afforded by a gradient.

Additionally, room heat is rarely cost-effective for a keeper with a pet snake or two. Relying on a single heating source for an entire room is also a high-risk proposition; if the heater or thermostat fails in the "on" position, the entire room may overheat.

Thermal Control Equipment

Some heating devices, such as heat lamps, are designed to operate at full capacity for the entire time that they are turned on. Such devices should not be used with thermostats – instead, care should be taken to calibrate the proper temperature.

Other devices, such as heat pads, heat tape and radiant heat panels are designed to be used with a regulating device to maintain the proper temperature, such as a thermostat or rheostat.

Rheostats

Rheostats are similar to light-dimmer switches, and they allow you to reduce the output of a heating device. In this way, you can dial in the proper temperature for the habitat.

The drawback to rheostats is that they only regulate the amount of power going to the device – they do not monitor the cage temperature or adjust the power flow automatically. In practice, even with the same level of power entering the device, the amount of heat generated by most heat sources varies over the course of the day.

If you set the rheostat so that it keeps the cage at the right temperature in the morning, it may become too hot by the middle of the day. Conversely, setting the proper temperature during the middle of the day may leave the morning temperatures too cool.

Care must be taken to ensure that the rheostat controller is not inadvertently bumped or jostled, causing the temperature to rise or fall outside of healthy parameters.

Thermostats

Thermostats are similar to rheostats, except that they also feature a temperature probe that monitors the temperature in the cage (or under the basking source). This allows the thermostat to adjust the power going to the device as necessary to maintain a predetermined temperature.

For example, if you place the temperature probe under a basking spot powered by a radiant heat panel, the thermostat will keep the temperature relatively constant under the basking site.

There are two different types of thermostats:

- "On-Off" thermostats work by cutting the power to the device when the probe's temperature reaches a given temperature.

    For example, if the thermostat were set to 85 degrees Fahrenheit (29 degrees Celsius), the heating device would turn off whenever the temperature exceeds this threshold. When the temperature falls below 85, the thermostat restores power to the unit, and the heater begins functioning again. This cycle will continue to repeat, thus maintaining the temperature within a relatively small range.

    Be aware that on-off thermostats have a "lag" factor, meaning that they do not turn off when the temperature reaches a given temperature. They turn off when the temperature is a few degrees *above* that temperature, and then turn back on when the temperate is a little *below* the set point. Because of this, it is important to avoid setting the temperature at the limits of your pet's acceptable range. Some premium models have an adjustable amount of threshold for this factor, which is helpful.

- Pulse proportional thermostats work by constantly sending pulses of electricity to the heater. By varying the rate of pulses, the amount of energy reaching the heating devices varies.

A small computer inside the thermostat adjusts this rate to match the set-point temperature as measured by the probe. Accordingly, pulse proportional thermostats maintain much more consistent temperatures than on-off thermostats do.

Lights should not be used with thermostats, as the constant flickering may stress your snake. Conversely, heat pads, heat tape, radiant heat panels and ceramic heat emitters should always be used with either a rheostat or, preferably, a thermostat to avoid overheating your snake.

Thermostat Failure
If used for long enough, all thermostats eventually fail. The question is will yours fail today or twenty years from now. While some thermostats fail in the "off" position, a thermostat that fails in the "on" position may overheat your snakes. Unfortunately, tales of entire collections being lost to a faulty thermostat are too common.

Accordingly, it behooves keepers to use high-quality thermostats. Some keepers use two thermostats, connected in series arrangement. By setting the second thermostat (the "backup thermostat") a few degrees higher than the setting used on the "primary thermostat," you safeguard yourself against the failure of either unit.

In such a scenario, the backup thermostat allows the full power coming to it to travel through to the heating device, as the temperature never reaches its higher set-point temperature.

However, if the first unit fails in the "on" position, the second thermostat will keep the temperatures from rising too high. The temperature will rise a few degrees in accordance with the higher set-point temperature, but it will not get hot enough to harm your snakes.

If the backup thermostat fails in the "on" position, the first thermostat retains control. If either fails in the "off" position, the temperature will fall until you rectify the situation, but a brief exposure to relatively cool temperatures is unlikely to be fatal.

Nighttime Heating

In most circumstances, you should provide your carpet python with a minor temperature drop at night. If the enclosure temperatures remain above about 65 degrees Fahrenheit (18 degrees Celsius) – about 70 degrees Fahrenheit (21 degrees Celsius) for young carpet pythons – you will not need to use a heat source at night. Instead, you can simply switch your heating device off at night, and turn it back on in the morning.

You can also plug the heating devices (and thermostats or rheostats) into a lamp-timer to automate the process. Some thermostats even have features that adjust the temperature of the thermostat during the night, lowering it to a specified level.

Those who must provide some type of nocturnal heat source can do so in a number of ways. Virtually any non-light-emitting heat source will function adequately in this capacity. Ceramic heating elements, radiant heat panels and heat pads, cables and tape all work well for supplying nocturnal heat.

Red lights can be used in reflector domes to provide heat as well. In fact, red lights can be used for heating during the day and night, but the cage will not be illuminated very well, unless other lights are incorporated during the day.

Incorporating Thermal Mass

One underutilized technique that is helpful for raising the temperature of a cage is to increase the cage's thermal mass.

Rocks, large water dishes and ceramic cage decorations are examples of items that may work in such contexts. These objects will absorb heat from the heat source, and then re-radiate heat into the habitat.

This changes the thermal characteristics of the habitat greatly. By simply adding a large rock, the cage may eventually warm up a few degrees.

Raising the cage's thermal mass also helps to reduce the cage's rate of cooling in the evening. By placing a thick rock under the basking light, it will absorb heat all day and radiate this heat after the lights turn off. Eventually it will reach room temperature, but this may take hours.

Always remember to monitor the cage surface temperatures and ambient temperatures regularly after changing the thermal characteristics of the cage. Pay special attention to the surface temperatures of items placed on or under a heat source.

Experiment with different amounts of thermal mass in the cage. Use items of different sizes, shapes and materials, and see how the cage temperatures change. In general, the more thermal mass in the cage, the more constant the temperature will stay.

Chapter 8: Lighting the Enclosure

Carpet pythons appear to thrive with only ambient room light – no supplemental light is necessary. However, high quality lighting will help showcase your pet's incredible colors and iridescence.

Because additional lighting may raise the cage temperatures, it is important to monitor the cage temperatures after adding or changing the type of light sources used. While fluorescent lights and small LEDs do not produce a lot of heat, they may generate enough to warm small cages to undesirable levels.

Lighting Options

A number of lighting options are available for interested keepers. While all of these options will make the cage brighter and accentuate your pet's coloration, some accomplish this goal better than others do.

Lights that produce a balanced spectrum with a high color-rendering index will make your snake look his best, but even economy bulbs will allow you to see your animal better.

Reptile-specific lights are not required, as carpet pythons do not require exposure to ultraviolet radiation to metabolize their dietary calcium and vitamin D, as many lizards and turtles do.

Heat Lamp Bulbs

In addition to warmth, heat lamps provide some supplemental illumination for the enclosure. However, as their primary purpose is to heat – not illuminate -- the enclosure, most bulbs used in heat lamps produce relatively poor light.

Wattage, price point and other factors drive product development and consumer choice – not light quality. Most incandescent bulbs produce very yellow, unbalanced light. Nevertheless, some manufacturers make incandescent bulbs that produce a relatively balanced spectrum, with respectable CRI.

Fluorescent Lights

Fluorescent bulbs are the best option for supplemental lighting. These lights produce higher quality light than incandescent bulbs do, and they do not produce very much heat.

You can use either linear fluorescent lights or "compact" fluorescent bulbs. Compact fluorescent bulbs can be used in heat lamps instead of incandescent bulbs (only for lighting purposes) while linear fluorescent lights require special ballasts.

LED Lights

Recently, LED technology has become much more affordable, and some keepers have begun using LED lights to brighten their enclosures.

The quality of light produced by LEDs offer surpasses that produced by any other lights, so these bulbs make a great choice, provided that their cost is not prohibitive.

Photoperiod

Provide your carpet python with a consistent day-night cycle to avoid causing him stress. Use a lamp timer to help keep the light cycle consistent, and make it unnecessary for you to do so manually.

Carpet pythons hailing from the northern reaches of their range will thrive best with a nearly balanced photoperiod (12 to 13 hours of light followed by 11 to 12 hours of darkness) throughout the year.

Subspecies hailing from farther south experience greater fluctuation in annual photoperiod, but they are still likely to thrive with a 12- or 13-hour photoperiod in captivity.

Breeding attempts, however, may be more successful if you adopt a fluctuating photoperiod, ranging from about 10 hours of light in the winter to 14 hours of light in the summer.

You can see the labial pits quite clearly in this photograph.

Chapter 9: Substrate and Furniture

Once you have purchased or constructed your carpet python's enclosure, you must place appropriate items inside it. In general, these items take the form of an appropriate substrate and the proper cage furniture.

Acceptable Substrates

Substrates are used to give your snake a comfortable surface on which to crawl and to absorb any liquids present.

There are a variety of acceptable choices, all of which have different benefits and drawbacks.

Paper Sheet Products

The easiest and safest substrates for carpet pythons are paper products in sheet form. While regular newspaper is the most common choice, paper towels, unprinted newspaper, butcher's paper or commercially produced cage liners are equally acceptable.

Paper substrates are very easy to maintain, but they do not last very long and must be completely replaced when they are soiled. Accordingly, they must be changed regularly -- at least once per week.

Use several layers of paper products to provide sufficient absorbency and a little bit of cushion for your snake.

Cypress Mulch

Cypress mulch is a popular substrate choice for many tropical species, including carpet pythons. The mulch looks attractive and holds humidity well.

Cypress mulch is available from most home improvement and garden centers, as well as pet supply retailers. No matter the source you use, be sure that the product contains 100 percent cypress mulch without any demolition or salvage content.

Fir (Orchid) Bark

Fir bark (sometimes called orchid bark) is an attractive substrate that absorbs and releases water effectively, making it well suited for carpet python maintenance.

The primary drawback to fir bark is its high cost.

Aspen Shavings

Aspen shavings are a popular substrate choice that works reasonably well with carpet pythons. Aspen shares most of the concerns that other particulate substrates do (ingestion hazards, increased labor), but many keepers use it successfully.

Aspen can be spot cleaned daily, but like most other particulate substrates, you must replace it completely every month. Aspen does not resist decay well, so it must be replaced frequently if you mist the cage regularly.

Soils

While not commonly used by many breeders or hobbyists, soil is an acceptable substrate. You can dig up your own soil, purchase organic soil products or mix your own blend.

Avoid products containing perlite, manure, fertilizers, pre-emergent herbicides or other additives. Sterilizing the soil before adding it to the enclosure is not strictly necessary, but it is probably wise to do so.

Substrates to Avoid

Some substrates are completely inappropriate for carpet python maintenance, and should be avoided. These include:

Pine Shavings – Pine shavings release volatile fumes that may lead to respiratory problems.

Cedar Shavings – Cedar shavings produce toxic fumes that may sicken or kill your snake. **Never use** cedar shavings for snake maintenance.

Sand – Sand is too dusty for carpet pythons and poorly suited for use in high-humidity habitats.

Gravel – You can use large gravel as a substrate, but its problems outweigh its benefits. Gravel must be washed when soiled, which is laborious and time consuming. Gravel is also quite heavy, which can cause headaches for the keeper.

Artificial Turf – Artificial turf is a poor substrate for most snakes, including carpet pythons.

Cage Furniture

In addition to a water bowl (discussed in chapter 12) and substrate, you must provide your snake with hiding opportunities to keep him feeling secure. Hiding places are critical for your snake's well-being and are in no way optional.

In addition to hiding spots, you can also add plants and climbing perches to the habitat. These are not strictly necessary, but they may provide your snake with a higher quality of life.

Hiding Spots

You can use a variety of items to create your snake's hiding spot, from commercially produced, decorative items to a crumpled piece of newspaper.

To a large extent, you can let your own preferences guide your choice. You simply need to ensure the hiding spots you offer are safe, are either easy to clean or cheap enough to replace regularly, and fit the snake snuggly.

Ideally, you should provide at least one hiding spot on the warm side of the cage, and one hiding spot on the cool side of the cage.

Commercial Hide Boxes
Commercial hide boxes come in a wide variety of shapes, sizes and styles. Opt for those constructed from non-porous materials (ceramic or plastic) and designed to fit your snake snuggly.

Plastic Storage Boxes
While not that attractive, small, opaque storage boxes make functional hiding places. Simply discard the lid to the container, flip the tub upside down and cut an entrance hole in the side.

Plant Saucers
The saucers designed to collect the water that overfills potted plants make excellent hiding locations. Just as with a plastic storage box, you simply need to flip a plant saucer upside down and cut a small opening in the side for a door. Clay or plastic saucers can be used, but clay saucers are hard to cut. If you punch an entrance hole into a clay saucer, you must sand or grind down the edges to prevent hurting your snake.

Plates
Plastic, paper or ceramic plates make good hiding locations for small carpet pythons in cages that use particulate substrates. This will allow the snake to burrow up under the plate through the substrate, and hide in a very tight space. Such hiding places also make it very easy to access your snake while he is hiding.

Cardboard Boxes
While you must discard and replace them anytime they become soiled, small cardboard boxes can make suitable hide boxes. Be sure to select one of the proper size, to ensure your snake feels safe while he is inside.

Commercial "Half-Logs"

Many pet stores sell U-shaped pieces of wood that resemble half of a hollow log. While these are sometimes attractive looking items, they are not appropriate hide spots when used as intended. The U-shaped construction means that the snake will not feel the top of the hide when he is laying inside. These hides can be functional if they are partially buried, thus reducing the height of the hide.

Cork Bark

Real bark cut from cork oak (*Quercus suber*) trees, "cork bark" is a wonderful looking decorative item that can be implemented in a variety of ways. Usually cork bark is available in tube shape or in flat sheets. Flat pieces are better for smaller carpet pythons, although exceptionally large snakes may be able to use tubular sections adequately. Flat pieces should only be used with particulate, rather than sheet-like substrates so that the snake can get under them easily.

Cork bark may be slightly difficult to clean, as its surface contains numerous indentations and crevices. Use hot water, soap and a sturdy brush to remove dirt and debris.

Paper Towel Tubes

Small sections of paper towel tubes make suitable hiding spots for small carpet pythons, although the snakes quickly become too large for such hides. They do not last very long, so they require frequent replacement. They often work best if flattened slightly.

Newspaper or Paper Towels

Several sheets of newspaper or paper towels placed on top of the substrate (whether sheet-like or particulate) make suitable hiding spots. Many professional breeders use paper-hiding spaces because it is such a simple and economically feasible solution. Some keepers crumple a few of the sheets to give the stack of paper more height.

Unusual Items

Some keepers like to express their individuality by using unique or unusual items as hiding spots. Some have used handmade ceramic items, while others have used skulls or turtle shells. If the four primary criteria previously discussed are met, there is no reason such items will not make suitable hiding spaces.

Humid Hides

In addition to security, snakes also derive another benefit from many of their hiding spaces in the wild. Most hiding places feature higher humidity than the surrounding air.

By spending a lot of time in such places, snakes are able to avoid dehydration in habitats where water is scarce. Additionally, time spent in these humid retreats aids in the shedding process. You should take steps to provide similar opportunities in captivity.

Humid hides can be made by placing damp sphagnum moss in a plastic container. The moss should not be saturated, but merely damp. You can also use damp paper towels or newspaper to increase the humidity of a hide box.

Some keepers prefer to keep humid hides in the habitat at all times, while others use them periodically – usually preceding shed cycles. Humid hides should never be the only hides available to the snake. Always use them in addition to dry hides.

Plants

While not absolutely necessary for sound husbandry, both live and artificial plants provide additional visual barriers for your snake and help to increase the complexity of the cage. They can also increase the aesthetic appeal of the habitat.

Artificial plants are simpler to select, install and maintain than live plants are, but live plants help to maintain good air quality and raise the humidity of the habitat.

Artificial plants require relatively little effort to install. Simply rinse them off and add them to the cage in a visually pleasing manner. Live plants, on the other hand, are often coated with pesticides or plagued by insects, so more effort is required before placing them in the habitat.

Always wash live plants before placing them in the enclosure to help remove any pesticide residues. It is also wise to discard the potting soil used for the plant and replace it with fresh soil, which you know contains no pesticides, perlite or fertilizer.

While you can plant cage plants directly in soil substrates, this complicates maintenance and makes it difficult to replace the substrate regularly. Accordingly, it is generally preferable to keep the plant in some type of container. Be sure to use a catch tray under the pot, so that water draining from the container does not flow into the cage.

You must use care to select a species that will thrive in your snake's enclosure. For example, plants that require direct sunlight will perish in the relatively dim light of the cage.

Instead, you must choose plants that will thrive in shaded conditions. Similarly, because you will be misting the cage regularly, and trying to keep the internal environment as humid as possible, few succulents or other plants adapted to arid habitats will live in a carpet python enclosure.

Some of the most common choices that are likely safe and well suited for your carpet python's enclosures include:

- Devil's Ivy (*Pothos* spp.)
- Small fig trees (*Ficus* spp.)
- Small umbrella trees (*Schefflera arboricola*)
- Split-leaf philodendrons (*Monstera deliciosa*)
- Assorted ferns (especially *Pteridophytas* spp.)
- Peace lilies (*Spathiphyllum* spp.)
- Pawpaws (*Asimina* spp.)
- *Neoregelia* bromeliads
- *Aechmea* bromeliads

Perches

Carpet pythons are semi-arboreal snakes that will appreciate and use perches in their enclosure.

You can purchase climbing branches from pet and craft stores, or you can collect them yourself. When collecting your own branches, try to use branches that are still attached to trees (make sure you always obtain permission before removing them). Such branches will harbor fewer insects and other invertebrate pests than dead branches will.

Many different types of branches can be used in carpet python cages. Most non-aromatic hardwoods suffice. See the chart below for specific recommendations.

Always wash branches with plenty of hot water and a stiff, metal-bristled scrub brush to remove as much dirt, dust and fungus as possible before placing them in your snake's cage. Clean stubborn spots with a little bit of dish soap, but be sure to rinse them thoroughly afterwards.

It is also advisable to sterilize branches before placing them in a cage. The easiest way to do so is by placing the branch in a 300-degree oven for about 15 minutes. Doing so should kill the vast majority of pests and pathogens lurking inside the wood.

Some keepers like to cover their branches with a water-sealing product. This is acceptable if a non-toxic product is used and the branches are allowed to air dry for several days before being placed in the cage. However, as branches are relatively easy to replace, it is not necessary to seal them if you plan to replace them.

You can often place branches diagonally across the enclosure, in such a way that alleviates the need for direct attachment to the cage. However, horizontal branches will require secure points of attachment so they do not fall and injure your pet.

You can attach the branches to the cage in a variety of different ways. Be sure to make it easy to remove the branches as necessary, so you can clean them easily.

You can use hooks and eye-screws to suspend branches, which allows for quick and easy removal, but it is only applicable for cages with walls that will accept and support the eye-screws. You can also make "closet rod holders" by cutting a slot into small PVC caps, which are attached to the cage frame.

Many carpet pythons spend a significant portion of their life perching.

Recommended Tree Species for Perches

Recommended Species

Maple trees (*Acer* spp.)

Oak trees (*Quercus* spp.)

Walnut trees (*Juglans* spp.)

Ash trees (*Fraxinus* spp.)

Dogwood trees (*Cornus* spp.)

Sweetgum trees (*Liquidambar stryaciflua*)

Crepe Myrtle trees (*Lagerstroemia* spp.)

Willow trees (*Salix* spp.)

Tuliptrees (*Liriodendron tulipifera*)

Pear trees (*Pyrus* spp.)

Apple trees (*Malus* spp.)

Manzanitas (*Arctostaphylos* spp.)

Species to Avoid

Cherry trees (*Prunus* spp.)

Pine trees (*Pinus* spp.)

Cedar trees (*Cedrus* spp., etc.)

Juniper trees (*Juniperus* spp.)

Poison ivy / oak (*Toxicodendron* spp.)

Chapter 10: Maintaining the Captive Habitat

Now that you have acquired your snake and set up the enclosure, you must develop a protocol for maintaining his habitat. While your carpet python's habitat will require major maintenance every month or so, it will only require minor maintenance on a daily basis.

In addition to designing a husbandry protocol, you must embrace a record-keeping system to track your snake's growth and health.

Cleaning and Maintenance Procedures

Once you have decided on the proper enclosure for your pet, you must keep your snake fed, hydrated and ensure that the habitat stays in proper working order to keep him healthy and comfortable.

Some tasks must be completed each day, while others are should be performed weekly, monthly or annually.

Daily
- Monitor the ambient and surface temperatures of the habitat.
- Ensure that the snake's water bowl is full of clean water.
- Ensure that the snake has not defecated or produced urates in the cage. If he has, you must clean the cage.
- Ensure that the lights, latches and other moving parts are in working order.
- Verify that your snake is acting normally and appears healthy. You do not need to handle him to do so.
- Ensure that the humidity and ventilation are at appropriate levels.

Weekly
- Feed your snake (this may not be necessary each week).
- Empty, wash and refill the water container.
- Change any sheet-like substrate.
- Clean the walls of the enclosure.

- Remove your snake (you can remove the perch with the snake if your snake is not easily handled) and inspect him for any injuries, parasites or signs of illness.

Monthly
- Break down the cage completely, remove and discard the substrate.
- Clean the entire cage from top to bottom.
- Sterilize the water dish and any other plastic or ceramic furniture in a mild bleach solution.
- Measure and weigh your snake (if your snake is not easy to handle, note the weight of his perch so that you can weigh him without removing him from the perch in the future).
- Soak your snake for about 1 hour (recommended, but not imperative).
- Photograph your snake (recommended, but not imperative).

Annually
- Visit the veterinarian to ensure that your snake is in good health.
- Replace the batteries in your thermometers and any other devices that use them.

Cleaning a snake's cage or an item from his cage is relatively simple. Regardless of the way it became soiled or its constituent materials, the basic process is the same:

1. Rinse the object
2. Using a scrub brush or sponge and soapy water, remove any organic debris from the object.
3. Rinse the object thoroughly.
4. Disinfect the object.
5. Re-rinse the object.
6. Dry the object.

Chemicals & Tools

A variety of chemicals and tools are necessary for reptile care. Save yourself some time by purchasing dedicated cleaning products and keeping them in the same place that you keep your tools.

Scrub Brushes or Sponges

It helps to have a few different types of scrub brushes and sponges on hand for scrubbing and cleaning different items. Use the least abrasive sponge or brush suitable for the task to prevent wearing out cage items prematurely. Do not use abrasive materials on glass or acrylic surfaces. Steel-bristled brushes work well for scrubbing coarse, wooden items, such as branches.

Spatulas and Putty Knives

Spatulas, putty knives and similar tools are often helpful for cleaning reptile cages. For example, urates (which are typically insoluble in water) often become stuck on cage walls or furniture. Instead of trying to dissolve them with harsh chemicals, just scrape them away with a sturdy plastic putty knife.

Small Vacuums

Small, handheld vacuums are very helpful for sucking up the dust left behind from substrates. They are also helpful for cleaning the cracks and crevices around the cage doors. A shop vacuum, with suitable hoses and attachments, can also be helpful.

Steam Cleaners

Steam cleaners are very effective for sterilizing cages, water bowls and durable cage props after they have been cleaned. In fact, steam is often a better choice than chemical disinfectants, as it will not leave behind a toxic residue. Never use a steam cleaner near your snake, the plants in his cage or any other living organisms.

Soap

Use a gentle, non-scented dish soap. Antibacterial soap is preferred, but not necessary. Most people use far more soap than is necessary -- a few drops mixed with a quantity of water is usually sufficient to help remove surface pollutants.

Bleach
Bleach (diluted to one-half cup per gallon of water) makes an excellent disinfectant. Be careful not to spill any on clothing, carpets or furniture, as it is likely to discolor the objects.

Always be sure to rinse objects thoroughly after using bleach and be sure that you cannot detect any residual odor. Bleach does not work as a disinfectant when in contact with organic substances; accordingly, items must be cleaned before you can disinfect them.

Veterinarian Approved Disinfectant
Many commercial products are available that are designed to be safe for their pets. Consult with your veterinarian about the best product for your situation, its method of use and its proper dilution.

Avoid Phenols
Always avoid cleaners that contain phenols, as they are extremely toxic to some reptiles. In general, do not use household cleaning products to avoid exposing your pet to toxic chemicals.

Keeping Records

It is important to keep records regarding your pet's health, growth and feeding, as well as any other important details. In the past, reptile keepers would do so on small index cards or in a notebook. In the modern world, technological solutions may be easier. For example, you can use your computer or mobile device to keep track of the pertinent info about your pet.

You can record as much information about your pet as you like, and the more information to you record, the better. But minimally, you should record the following:

Pedigree and Origin Information
Be sure to record the source of your snake, the date on which you acquired him and any other data that is available. Breeders will often provide customers with information regarding the sire, dam, date of birth, weights and feeding records, but other sources will rarely offer comparable data.

Feeding Information
Record the date of each feeding, as well as the type of food item(s) offered. It is also helpful to record any preferences you may observe or any meals that are refused.

Weights and Length
Because you look at your pet frequently, it is difficult to appreciate how quickly he is (or isn't) growing. Accordingly, it is important to track his size diligently.

Weigh your carpet python with a high quality digital scale. The scale must be sensitive to 1-gram increments to be useful for very small pythons, but scales that measure weight in 5-gram increments are sufficient for larger animals.

It is often easiest to use a dedicated "weighing container" with a known weight to measure your snake. This way, you can simply place him in the container and place the entire container on the scale. Subtract the weight of the container to obtain the weight of your snake.

If you like, you can measure your snake's length as well, but this is rather difficult and rarely provides an accurate measurement.

Maintenance Information
Record all of the noteworthy events associated with your pet's care. While it is not necessary to note that you misted the cage each day, it is appropriate to record the dates on which you changed the substrate or sterilized the cage.

Whenever you purchase new equipment, supplies or caging, note the date and source. This not only helps to remind you when you purchased the items, but it may help you track down a source for the items in the future, if necessary.

Breeding Information
If you intend to breed your snake, you should record all details associated with pre-breeding conditioning, cycling, introductions, matings, copulations, ovulation and partruition.

Record Keeping Samples

The following are two different examples of suitable recording systems.

The first example is reminiscent of the style employed by many with large collections. Because such keepers often have numerous animals, the notes are very simple, and require a minimum amount of writing or typing.

The second example demonstrates a simple approach better suited for those with a single pet: keeping notes on paper. Such notes could be taken in a notebook or journal, or you could type directly into a word processor. It does not matter *how* you keep records, just that you *do* keep records.

ID Number: 44522		Genus: Species: Subspecies:	Morelia spilota cheynei	Gender: DOB:	Male 6/20/13	CARD #2
6.30.15 1 Small Rat	7.13.15 Blue	7.23.15 Shed	8.02.15 1 Small Rat	8.27.15 Blue		
7.05.15 1 Small Rat	7.15.15 Soak	7.24.15 1 Small Rat	8.8.15 1 Small Rat	8.29.15 Soaked / Sterilized Cage		
7.10.15 1 Small Rat	7.16.15 Soak	7.29.15 1 Small Rat	8.16.15 1 Small Rat			

Date	Notes
4-22-13	Acquired "Clyde" the jungle carpet python from a breeder named Mark at the in-town reptile expo. Mark explained that Clyde's scientific name is Morelia spilota cheynei. Cost was $180. Mark was not sure what sex Clyde is. Mark said he purchased him in March, but he does not know the exact date.
4-23-13	Clyde spent the night in the container I bought him in. I purchased a small snake cage, heat lamp and water dish at the pet store. Bought the

	thermometer at the hardware store next door and ordered a non-contact thermometer online. I am using old food containers for his hiding place.
6-27-13	*Clyde ate a small adult mouse.*
6-30-13	*The bulge from Clyde's last meal has disappeared, and he looks hungry again!*
7-1-13	*I fed Clyde another small mouse.*
7-3-13	*When I looked at Clyde this morning, his eyes were bright blue! I guess he is going to shed his skin soon. I am excited to see how beautiful his colors are afterwards.*

Chapter 11: Feeding Carpet Pythons

For new keepers, few aspects of carpet python care are as exciting as feeding their pet. However, feeding your carpet python properly entails more than just purchasing a rodent and tossing it in your snake's cage periodically.

Instead, you must select the food items carefully, present the food items in a safe manner and do so on an appropriate schedule.

Prey Species

Generally speaking, the best food items for your carpet python are commercially reared rodents – specifically rats and mice.

While there are some minor nutritional differences between rats and mice, both make suitable staples for your pet. It is likely better to feed your animal fully furred, weaned rodents, rather than newborns, so it makes sense to feed your snake mice until it is large enough to consume fully furred rats.

While it is possible to feed other prey species – notably ducks, chicks and rabbits – to your snake, these feeder items do not appear to offer any additional benefits to you or your snake and they present additional challenges.

While most pet stores carry feeder mice and feeder rats, relatively few carry ducks, chicks or rabbits in sizes appropriate for carpet pythons. With sufficient effort, most hobbyists can track down a source for small rabbits, ducks or chicks, but there is little upside to justify extraordinary efforts.

Carpet pythons often spend long periods of time laying in ambush postures.

In fact, some of these alternative food items have minor drawbacks. For example, snakes that eat birds often produce soft, offensive smelling feces. Additionally, snakes that subsist on bird-based diets are at an increased risk of contracting *Salmonella*.

While young carpet pythons feed on lizards and other ectothermic species in the wild, these animals should not be offered to captive snakes, as they may transmit pathogens or parasites to your pet.

Prey Size

Try to feed your pet prey items that are about 1.25 to 1.5 times his midbody diameter. They should create a modest, but distinct lump in the snake's body once swallowed.

Most newborns are large enough to consume hopper (fully furred) mice, and within no time, they are large enough to handle small adult mice.

By the time they reach 1 year of age, most carpet pythons can handle large adult mice or hopper (fully furred) rats. Medium to large rats are appropriate for most adults, although small individuals may be better served by small rats.

Realize that rodent size classes are somewhat arbitrarily defined – one breeder's "large" may be another's "medium."

Live, Fresh Killed or Frozen

Carpet pythons are perfectly capable of killing small rodents, birds or lizards, but these animals can and do fight back. Sometimes, these conflicts lead to serious injuries.

For example, snakes occasionally grab their prey incorrectly, which can allow the prey animal to bite or scratch the snake. In some cases, these wounds can be quite severe.

There is also the ethical problem of allowing a rodent to be stalked, bitten, constricted and killed by a snake when it is not necessary to do so – the vast majority of carpet pythons will readily accept dead prey. A quick, effective form of euthanasia is clearly preferable to such a traumatic death – rodents are no less deserving of humane treatment than any other animal kept in captivity.

Accordingly, it is always preferable to feed your snake pre-killed prey items. Whenever possible, these food items should also be of the frozen-thawed variety, which affords some protection against parasites and pathogens.

Fortunately, as they are both safer and more convenient than the alternatives, frozen rodents are widely available to hobbyists.

How to Offer Food Safely

Many (perhaps most) carpet python bites result from feeding mistakes. Fortunately, such mistakes are easy to avoid by following proper feeding practices.

Begin by thawing your feeding rodent beforehand. Do so by placing the rodent in warm water or by leaving it out room temperature. Never attempt to thaw a rodent in the microwave.

Once it has thawed completely, remove any distractions and pick up the rodent with your feeding tongs before opening the cage.

Once you open the enclosure, present the item a few inches from the snake's head. With luck, the snake will quickly bite the rodent and begin constricting it. Release the rodent, withdraw your hand and close the cage.

Realize that snakes are often hyperalert after consuming a food item, so you should avoid opening the cage (unless you intend to feed a second prey item) for several hours following meals.

Never reach into your snake's cage while your hands smell like mice, rats, birds, lizards or other potential prey, as an excited carpet python may mistake your hand for a delicious food item.

Feeding Quantity and Frequency

Most keepers offer young snakes one appropriately sized prey item per week. However, this may represent surplus calories for mature specimens, which can cause them to gain weight and experience health problems. Accordingly, it is sometimes necessary to feed mature snakes less frequently or employ occasional week-long-fasts.

Nevertheless, keepers utilize a wide variety of feeding schedules. Some prefer to offer relatively small prey items more frequently (perhaps once every 3 to 5 days), while others prefer to feed larger meals less frequently (perhaps once every 10 to 14 days). Still others may feed two small prey items at each feeding.

Any of these schedules will work – the important thing is to monitor your snake's weight and make adjustments as necessary.

Avoiding Regurgitation

Just like humans, snakes may regurgitate or vomit food items in response to a variety of stimuli, including toxins, stress and temperature extremes.

Accordingly, it is important to feed your snake only the highest quality rodents, avoid causing the animal stress (especially right after meals) and maintaining the habitat within the correct temperature range.

Vomiting and regurgitation not only saddle the keeper with unpleasant clean up duties, they are very hard on the snakes body. Among other problems, vomiting can lead to dehydration and additional stress.

Give snakes that vomit at least one full week before offering food again. One of the biggest mistakes keepers make when dealing with a snake that has regurgitated is that they try to make up for the lost meal too quickly. This stresses the snake's digestive system and can lead to long-term, chronic problems

Chapter 12: Water and Humidity

Like most other animals, carpet pythons require drinking water to remain healthy. However, the relative humidity (the amount of water in the air) is also an important factor in their health.

While both drinking water and humid air help to keep carpet pythons hydrated, the moisture in the air also helps to keep their skin healthy and helps prevent respiratory problems from developing.

Providing Drinking Water

Provide your pet with a dish full of clean, fresh drinking water at all times.

While it is acceptable to offer the snakes a bowl that will accommodate the snake, it is not necessary. Many keepers use bowls with 4- to 6-inch diameters. Be sure to avoid filling large containers too high, as they are apt to overflow if the snake crawls into the bowl.

Carpet pythons are heavy, muscular animals that may tip their water bowl, so use a bowl heavy or wide enough that the snake will not tip it inadvertently. Plastic trays, such as clean cat litter pans, also work very well for supplying your snake with water.

Be sure to check the water dish daily and ensure that the water is clean. Empty, wash and refill the water dish any time it becomes contaminated with substrate, shed skin, urates or feces.

Some keepers prefer to use dechlorinated or bottled water for their snakes; however, untreated tap water is used by many keepers with no ill effects.

Maintaining Proper Cage Humidity

Most carpet pythons inhabit humid regions and they require similarly high humidity in captivity. Even those carpet pythons that hail from dry macrohabitats spend much of their time in relatively humid microhabitats.

As a rule of thumb, carpet pythons are comfortable at humidity levels of about 50 to 70 percent.

While experienced keepers are often successful maintaining suitable humidity levels without precise measurements, beginners should monitor the humidity. Beginning snake keepers should consider acquiring and utilizing a hygrometer in their snake's cage to measure the relative humidity level.

Be aware though, economy "stick-on" hygrometers seldom yield accurate results. Many digital thermometers are capable of measuring relative humidity in addition to temperature.

Because the natural humidity level varies greatly from one snake keeper's residence to another, different keepers will need to use different strategies for maintaining suitable humidity levels. It is often necessary to experiment with different strategies to arrive at the best solution for your situation.

If you use an air conditioner in your home during the summer or the heater during the winter, you may find that your cages dry out faster than normal. Both such units reduce the humidity of the air in your home, which will tend to draw moisture out of the cage. Accordingly, you may need to vary your approach with the season.

There are two primary ways of increasing the relative humidity in your pet's cage: Add more water or restrict the amount of water that is allowed to evaporate from the cage.

Adding Water
It is often possible to achieve suitable humidity levels by simply incorporating a large water dish into the habitat. The volume of water is not as important as the surface area of the water. In other words, a shallow, wide dish will raise the cage humidity more than a narrow, deeper water bowl will.

Placing the water dish under a heat lamp or over a heating pad will help accelerate the evaporation rate, but it will require you to refill the water dish more frequently.

You can also dampen the substrate to elevate the humidity level inside the cage. The dampened substrate will slowly release water into the air in the cage, thus elevating the humidity. This works best with moisture-retaining substrates, such as cypress mulch or orchid bark. However, you can also dampen newspaper and many other paper-based substrates.

Misting

Another way to add water to the cage is by misting the substrate and interior surfaces of the enclosure with lukewarm water.

It is perfectly safe to spray your snake (gently) with clean, lukewarm water, but be aware that some snakes do not like to be sprayed. Avoid spraying your snake in the face, as this often results in a defensive strike.

Snake that react badly to misting may be more comfortable when "rained" on, rather than misted. You can accomplish this by misting the ceiling of the cage (this obviously isn't possible with screened cage lids – yet another reason to favor front-opening, reptile cages rather than aquaria). The water will tend to collect on the surface, and fall down onto the snake in large drops.

Keepers with one snake will usually find a simple, handheld spray bottle to be sufficient, but those with several snakes likely prefer the convenience offered by a compressed-air sprayer.

Always allow the standing water droplets to evaporate or soak into the substrate between mistings – the cage should not stay wet for extended periods of time.

In addition to increasing the cage humidity temporarily, misting often causes carpet pythons to become active. This benefits them by encouraging exercise and mental stimulation; it may also cause them to defecate. Misting can even be used to elicit mating behavior.

One drawback to misting cages is that the water droplets can leave unsightly spots on glass surfaces. Using water with a low-mineral content often helps eliminate this problem (however, distilled water should not be used for snake maintenance).

Restricting Airflow

Cages with excess ventilation (such as those featuring screened lids) may allow too much water to evaporate from the cage. To prevent this from happening, you can attach a piece of glass or plastic to a portion of the screened areas of the cage. Only cover as much of the cage as is necessary to raise the humidity to avoid creating stagnant air in the cage.

Live Plants

Live plants provide another way to raise cage humidity. Plants engage in a process known as transpiration, in which they draw water from the ground and release it via small openings in the plant leaves.

Additionally, live plants can serve as "canaries in the coal mine." For example, if your plant starts to wilt, it does not have enough water, which also means that humidity level in the cage is probably not high enough. By taking care of the plant – which will succumb to dehydration faster than the snake will – the keeper is more likely to maintain proper humidity levels.

Live plants also provide cover for the snake, which is especially helpful when raising young animals.

You must use care to select plants that will thrive in your carpet python's enclosure, otherwise you will need to replace them constantly. For example, you should avoid species that require direct sunlight, as they will perish in the relatively dim light in your snake's enclosure. Instead, choose plants that will thrive in shaded conditions.

Similarly, because you will be misting the cage regularly and trying to keep the internal environment as humid as possible, it is wise to avoid succulents or other plants adapted to arid habitats.

No matter what plants you chose, be sure to wash them before placing them in the enclosure, to help remove any pesticide residues that are present. It is also wise to discard the potting soil used for the plant and replace it with fresh soil, which you know contains no pesticides, perlite or fertilizer.

Because snakes will not chew on the plants in their cage as lizards or turtles do, you can use plants that may be poisonous if eaten. However, it is still wise to avoid species that exude skin-irritating saps or feature spines, prickles or thorns.

Soaking Snakes

In addition to providing drinking water, many keepers soak their carpet pythons periodically in a tub of clean, lukewarm water. Soaking is helpful tool for the husbandry of many snakes, especially those that hail from humid habitats.

In addition to ensuring that your snake remains adequately hydrated, soaks help to remove dirt and encourage complete, problem-free sheds. It is not necessary to soak your snake if it remains adequately hydrated, but most carpet pythons benefit from an occasional soak.

Soaks should last a maximum of about one hour, and be performed no more often than once per week (unless the snake is experiencing shedding difficulties).

When soaking your snake, the water should not be very deep. Never make your snake swim to keep its head above water. Ideally, snakes should be soaked in containers with only enough water to cover their back. This should allow your snake to rest comfortably with its head above water.

It is important to monitor your snake while he is soaking -- never leave a pet unattended while he is in a container of water. If your snake defecates in the water, be sure to rinse him off with clean water before returning him to his cage.

Chapter 13: Interacting with Your Carpet Python

Many keepers enjoy handling pet snakes; assuming that they do not occur too frequently, gentle, brief handling sessions are unlikely to stress your pet. In fact, it is necessary to handle your snake from time to time – not only so that you can move him while you clean his cage, but also to monitor his health.

Every carpet python is an individual, which means that different snakes respond differently when interacting with their keeper. Most captive raised carpet pythons eventually learn to tolerate gentle handling, but some remain defensive throughout their lives.

No matter what side of the spectrum your snake falls on, you must be able to handle your pet when necessary – even if he is very defensive.

Picking Up a Carpet Python

Try to move with a purpose once you open the cage door. Don't stare at your snake for 15 minutes as you try to work up your nerve. This often makes snakes feel insecure, which leads to defensive behaviors.

Pick up your carpet python by gently sliding your fingers underneath his body and lifting him into the air. Small snakes can be supported adequately with one hand, but two hands are necessary for lifting medium or large specimens.

Young carpet pythons can be nippy, but they usually calm down over time with frequent interaction. The bites of young carpet pythons are harmless (many will not even break the skin of your fingers), but they still make many beginning keepers nervous.

If you would like to avoid the bites and strikes of small carpet pythons, you can cover the snake with a paper towel before picking him up. This usually keeps the snake calmer and discourages them from biting.

Alternatively, you can use a snake hook (or an improvised version thereof) to lift your snake from the ground. If necessary, you can rely almost entirely on a snake hook for moving your snake around.

You can simply lift him out of his cage, place him in a temporary cage while you clean his habitat, and then (using the hook), repeat the process in reverse. This means that you needn't come into direct contact with an aggressive carpet python during the course of routine maintenance (you will still need to handle your snake to inspect his health).

No matter how aggressive the snake is, you should avoid "pinning" him behind the head, as some keepers do with venomous species. Inexperienced keepers often apply too much pressure to the snake's neck, which can have tragic consequences.

Gloves provide another alternative for those who desire some protection while handling their carpet python. Virtually any type of thick glove will work (batting gloves, work gloves, welding gloves, etc.), as the teeth of young carpet pythons are not very long.

Gloves only provide a small amount of protection against larger specimens. The longer teeth of adults may be able to penetrate gloves that the smaller teeth of young specimens cannot, and adults are also able to strike a lot farther than small specimens can. Large individuals can strike far enough to reach your arms, torso or face, while the snake is in your hands.

Holding a Carpet Python

Now that you have picked up your carpet python, you must hold him in a way that prevents stress or injury.

The best way to hold a snake and keep it from feeling threatened is to provide it with plenty of support and allow it to crawl freely through your hands. Avoid restraining your snake or gripping it tightly with your hands, as this will cause it to feel like prey.

Instead, simply support its body weight, and allow it to crawl from one hand to the other.

Usually, your carpet python will grip your hands or arms, as though you were a tree. This can cause new keepers a bit of apprehension, but with time, you will become used to it.

Despite this tendency, it is always wise to handle the snake over a table or other object to prevent his from falling to the floor, should he make a sudden move.

Always be patient and gentle when transferring your carpet python to or from your hands. Never attempt to pry your pet from a perch or pull him by his tail. Instead, you can simply tickle his tail, which will usually cause him to release his grip and move forward.

Handling Your Snake Safely

Even tame carpet pythons must be handled safely. While they are unlikely to cause grave bodily harm, large specimens can certainly inflict a nasty bite. Accordingly, you must avoid placing the snake near your face (or anyone else's face).

Always be sure to avoid smelling like potential prey when handling carpet pythons, and refrain from handling snakes in the presence of unsupervised children or pets.

While few carpet pythons grow large enough to represent a constriction hazard to adult humans, it is not wise to tempt fate. Have another adult present when handling large or aggressive individuals and avoid placing your pet around your neck.

Handling Your Snake Responsibly

Always realize that you are responsible for your snake while you are holding it. Accidents can and do happen. Such occurrences are very bad for snakes, snake keepers and the entire snake-keeping hobby, and must be avoided.

Essentially, this means that you must keep your snake far enough away from other people that he cannot bite them, should he become frightened or startled. It is also worth mentioning that scared snakes may defecate or release urates – sometimes in a semi-projectile fashion.

Never handle your snake in a public situation. Do not take your snake to the park or to the local fast food restaurant. Your snake is not a toy, he does not appreciate "hanging out" in this manner, and it makes snake keepers everywhere look bad.

Snakes frighten many people and you should always be sensitive to this fact. Rather than playing into these fears, seek to educate people about snakes rather than shock them by bringing them to inappropriate events and locations.

In The Event of a Bite

If your carpet python bites you, remain calm. If it is a defensive bite, the snake will usually release its hold on your skin quickly. If this occurs, you can simply close the cage or return the snake to his enclosure.

After returning the snake to his cage, wash the wound thoroughly with soap and warm water. Consult your doctor if the bite is serious, if it will not stop bleeding or if you can feel teeth lodged in the wound.

If the snake does not release his grip (such as occurs in a feeding bite), the best thing to do is place him in a bucket of cold water. Most snakes will voluntarily let go after being submerged for a minute or two. As with a defensive bite, you should wash the wound, and contact your doctor if the wound is serious.

Transporting Your Pet

Although you should strive to avoid any unnecessary travel with your python, circumstances (such as illness) often demand that you do.

Strive to make the journey as stress-free as possible for your pet. This means protecting him from physical harm, as well as blocking out any stressful stimuli.

The best type of container to use when transporting your python is a plastic storage box. Add several ventilation holes to the container to provide suitable ventilation and be sure that the lid fits securely.

Place a few paper towels or some clean newspaper in the bottom of the box in case your snake defecate or discharge urates. It is also wise to crumple a few of the layers of newspaper, which will provide a place in which your snake can hide.

Cover the outside of the transport cage if you are not using an opaque container, which will prevent your pet from seeing the chaos occurring outside his container. Check up on your snake regularly, but avoid constantly opening the container to take a peak. A quick peak once every half-hour or so is more than sufficient.

Pay special attention to the enclosure temperatures while traveling. Use your digital thermometer to monitor the air temperatures inside the transportation container. Try to keep the temperatures in the mid-70s Fahrenheit (23 to 25 degrees Celsius) so that your pet will remain comfortable. Use the air-conditioning or heater in your vehicle as needed to keep the transport cage within this range (because you cannot control the thermal environment, it is not wise to take your snake with you on public transportation).

Keep your snake's transportation container stable while traveling. Do not jostle the container unnecessarily and always use a gentle touch when moving it. Never leave the container unattended.

Hygiene

Reptiles can carry *Salmonella* spp., *Escherichia coli* and several other zoonotic pathogens. Accordingly, it is imperative that you use good hygiene practices when handling reptiles.

Always wash your hands with soap and warm water each time you touch your pet, his habitat or the tools you use to care for him. Antibacterial soaps are preferred, but standard hand soap will suffice.

In addition to keeping your hands clean, you must also take steps to ensure your environment does not become contaminated with pathogens. In general, this means keeping your snake and any of the tools and equipment you use to maintain his habitat separated from your belongings.

Establish a safe place for preparing his food, storing equipment and cleaning his habitat. Make sure these places are far from the places in which you prepare your food and personal effects. Never wash cages or tools in kitchens or bathrooms that are used by humans.

Always clean and sterilize any items that become contaminated by the germs from your snake or his habitat.

This jungle carpet python is in a defensive pose.

Chapter 14: Common Health Concerns

Your carpet python cannot tell you when he is sick; reptiles endure illness stoically. This does not mean that injuries and illnesses do not cause them distress, but without expressive facial features, they do not *look* like they are suffering.

In fact, reptiles typically do not display symptoms until the disease has already reached an advanced state. Accordingly, it is important to treat injuries and illnesses promptly – often with the help of a qualified veterinarian –in order to provide your pet with the best chance of recovery.

Finding a Suitable Veterinarian

Carpet python keepers often find that it is more difficult to find a veterinarian to treat their snake than it is to find a vet to treat a cat or dog. Relatively few veterinarians treat reptiles, so it is important to find a reptile-oriented vet *before* you need one. There are a number of ways to do this:

- You can search veterinarian databases to find one that is local and treats reptiles.

- You can inquire with your dog or cat vet to see if he or she knows a qualified reptile-oriented veterinarian to whom he or she can refer you.

- You can contact a local reptile-enthusiast group or club. Most such organizations will be familiar with the local veterinarians.

- You can inquire with local nature preserves or zoos. Most will have relationships with veterinarians that treat reptiles and other exotic animals.

Those living in major metropolitan areas may find a vet reasonably close, but rural reptile keepers may have to travel considerable distances to find veterinary assistance.

If you do not have a reptile-oriented veterinarian within driving distance, you can try to find a conventional veterinarian who is willing to consult with a reptile-oriented veterinarian via the phone or internet.

These types of "two-for-one" visits may be expensive, as you will have to pay for both the actual visit and the consultation, but they may be your only option.

Reasons to Visit the Veterinarian

While snakes do not require vaccinations or similar routine treatments, they may require visits for other reasons. Anytime your snake exhibits signs of illness or suffers an injury, you must visit the veterinarian.

Visit your veterinarian when:

- You first acquire your snake. This will allow your veterinarian to familiarize himself or herself with your pet while it is presumably healthy. This gives him or her a baseline against which he or she can consider future deviations. Additionally, your veterinarian may be able to diagnose existing illnesses, before they cause serious problems.

- Your time your snake wheezes, exhibits labored breathing or produces a mucus discharge from its nostrils or mouth.

- Your snake produces soft or watery feces (soft feces are expected when snakes are fed some food items, such as birds. This is not necessarily cause for concern.). Intestinal prolapses also necessitate immediate veterinary care.

- Your snake suffers any significant injury. Common examples include thermal burns, friction damage to the rostral (nose) region or damaged scales.

- Reproductive issues occur, such as being unable to deliver young. If a snake appears nervous, agitated or otherwise stressed and unable to give birth, see your veterinarian immediately.

- Your snake fails to feed for an extended period. While many snakes fast from time to time – which is no cause for concern – a veterinarian should see any new snake that does not eat for 4 weeks. Snakes that have been in your care, and normally eat aggressively, may fast for longer than this without ill effects.

Ultimately, you must make all the decisions on behalf of your snake, so weigh the pros and cons of each veterinary trip carefully and make the best decision you can for your pet.

Just be sure that you always strive to act in his best interest.

Common Health Problems

While a wide variety of health problems can befall your snake, the majority will fall into one of the following categories.

Retained or Poor Sheds

From time to time, captive snakes fail to shed completely. This is particularly common among snakes that hail from high-humidity habitats, such as carpet pythons.

With proper husbandry, healthy snakes should produce one-piece sheds regularly (if the shed skin is broken in one or two places, but comes off easily, there is no cause for concern).

Retained sheds vary in their severity. Sometimes snakes simply fail to shed a small portion of scales, and other times, snakes may retain the majority of the old skin.

Retained sheds can cause health problems, particularly if they restrict blood flow. This is often a problem when a snake retains a bit of old skin near the tail tip.

If your snake sheds poorly, you must take steps to remove the old skin and review your husbandry to prevent the problem from happening again. If you are providing ideal husbandry parameters, and yet your snake still experiences poor sheds, consult your veterinarian to rule out illness.

The best way to remove retained sheds is by soaking your snake or placing him in a damp container for about an hour. After removing him, see if you can gently peel the skin off. Try to keep the skin in as few pieces as possible to make the job easier.

Do not force the skin off your snake if it will not come off easily; simply return him to his cage and repeat the process again in 12 to 24 hours. Usually, repeated soaks or time in a damp hide will loosen the skin sufficiently to flake off easily.

If repeated treatments do not yield results, consult your veterinarian. He may feel that the retained shed is not causing a problem, and advise you to leave it attached – it should come off with the snake's next shed. Alternatively, it if is causing a problem, the veterinarian can likely remove it.

Retained Spectacles

Spectacles are the clear scales that cover your snake's eyes. Sometimes, snakes fail to shed their spectacles, which can lead to serious medical problems in some cases.

Do not try to remove a retained spectacle yourself; simply keep the snake in a humid environment and take it to your veterinarian, who should be able to remove the retained scales relatively easily.

Respiratory Infections

Like humans, snakes can suffer from respiratory infections. Snakes with respiratory infections may exude fluid or mucus from their nose or mouth, be lethargic or refuse food. They may also spend excessive amounts of time basking on or under the heat source, in an effort to induce a "behavioral fever."

Bacteria, or, less frequently, fungi or parasites can cause respiratory infections. Additionally, cleaning products, perfumes, pet dander and other particulate matter can irritate a snake's respiratory tract.

Some infective bacteria and fungi are ubiquitous, and only become problematic when they overwhelm a snake's immune system. Other bacteria, as well as most viruses, are communicable, meaning that they are transmitted from one snake to another.

To reduce the chances of illnesses, keep your snake quarantined from other snakes, keep his enclosure exceptionally clean and be sure to provide the best husbandry possible, especially as it relates to temperature and humidity. You should also avoid stressing your snake by handling him too frequently or exposing him to chaotic situations.

Most respiratory infections require veterinary assistance. Your veterinarian will likely take samples of the mucus and have it analyzed to determine the causal agent. The veterinarian will then prescribe medications, such as antibiotics or antifungal medications, as appropriate.

It is imperative to carry out the actions prescribed by your veterinarian exactly as stated and keep your snake's stress level very low while he is healing, as stress can reduce immune function. You should also consider covering the front of his cage while he recovers.

Many snakes produce audible breathing sounds for a few days immediately preceding a shed cycle, which does not necessarily indicate a respiratory infection. This is rarely cause for concern and will resolve once the snake sheds. However, if you are in doubt, always seek veterinary attention.

"Mouth Rot"
Mouth rot – properly called stomatitis – is identified by noting discoloration, discharge or cheesy-looking material in the snake's

mouth. Mouth rot can be a serious illness, and requires the attention of your veterinarian.

While mouth rot can follow an injury (such as happens when a snake strikes the side of a glass cage) it can also arise from systemic illness. Your veterinarian will cleanse your snake's mouth and potentially prescribe an antibiotic.

Your veterinarian may recommend withholding food until the problem is remedied. Always be sure that snakes that are recovering from mouth rot are kept in immaculately clean habitats with ideal temperature gradients.

Internal Parasites
In the wild, most snakes carry some internal parasites. While it may not be possible to keep a snake completely free of internal parasites, it is important to keep these levels in check.

Consider any wild-caught snake to be parasitized until proven otherwise. While most captive bred snakes should have relatively few internal parasites, they can suffer from such problems as well.

Preventing parasites from building to pathogenic levels requires strict hygiene. Many parasites build up to dangerous levels when the snakes are kept in cages that are continuously contaminated from feces.

Most internal parasites that are of importance for snakes are transmitted via the fecal-oral route. This means that eggs (or a similar life stage) of the parasites are released with the feces. If the snake inadvertently ingests these, the parasites can develop inside the snake's body and cause increased problems. Such eggs are usually microscopic and easily lifted into the air, where they may stick to cage walls or land in the water dish. Later, when the snake flicks its tongue or drinks from the water dish, it ingests the eggs.

Internal parasites may cause your snake to vomit, pass loose stools, fail to grow or refuse food entirely. Other parasites may produce no symptoms at all, which illustrates the importance of routine examinations.

Your veterinarian will usually examine your snake's feces if he suspects internal parasites. By looking at the type of eggs inside the snake's feces, you veterinarian can determine which medication will treat the problem.

Many parasites are easily treated with anti-parasitic medications, but often, these medications must be given several times to eradicate the pathogens completely.

Some parasites may be transmissible to people, so always take proper precautions, including regular hand washing and keeping snakes and their cages away from kitchens and other areas where foods are prepared.

Examples of common internal parasites include roundworms, tapeworms and amoebas.

External Parasites

The primary external parasites that afflict snakes are ticks and snake mites. Ticks are rare on captive bred animals, but wild caught snakes may be plagued by dozens of the small arachnids.

Ticks should be removed manually. Using tweezers grasp the tick as close as possible to the snake's skin and pull with steady, gentle pressure. Do not place anything over the tick first, such as petroleum jelly, or carry out any other "home remedies," such as burning the tick with a match. Such techniques may cause the tick to inject more saliva (which may contain diseases or bacteria) into the snake's body.

Drop the tick in a jar of isopropyl alcohol to ensure it is killed. It is a good idea to bring these to your veterinarian for analysis. Do not contact ticks with your bare hands, as many species can transmit disease to humans.

Mites are another matter entirely. While ticks are generally large enough to see easily, mites are about the size of a pepper flake. Whereas very bad tick infestations number in the dozens, mite infestations may include thousands of individual parasites.

Mites may afflict wild caught snakes, but, as they are not confined to a small cage, such infestations are somewhat self-limiting. However, in captivity, mite infestations can approach plague proportions.

After a female mite feeds on a snake, she drops off and finds a safe place (such as a tiny crack in a cage or among the substrate) to deposit her eggs. After the eggs hatch, they travel back to your snake (or to other snakes in your collection) where they feed and perpetuate the lifecycle.

Whereas a few mites may represent little more than an inconvenience to the snake, a significant infection can stress them considerably. In extreme cases, they may even lead to anemia and eventual death. This is particularly true for small or young animals. Additionally, mites may transmit disease from one snake to another.

There are a number of different methods for eradicating a mite infestation. In each case, there are two primary steps that must be taken: You must eradicate the snake's parasites, and eradicate the parasites in the snake's environment (which includes the room in which the cage resides).

It is relatively simple to remove mites from a snake. When mites get wet, they die. However, mites are protected by a thick, waxy exoskeleton that stimulates the formation of an air bubble.

This means that you cannot place your snake in water to drown the mites. The mites will simply hide under the snake's scales, protected by the air bubble.

To defeat this waxy cuticle, you can simply add a few drops of liquid soap to the water. The soap will lower the surface tension of water, allowing it to creep under the snake's scales. Additionally, the soap disrupts the surface tension of the water, preventing the air bubble from forming.

Soaking your snake is the slightly soapy water for about one hour will kill most of the mites on his body. Use care when doing so, but try to arrange the water level and container so that most of the snake's body is below the water.

While the snake is soaking, perform a thorough cage cleaning. Remove everything from the cage, including water dishes, substrates and cage props. Sterilize all impermeable cage items, and discard the substrate and all porous cage props. Vacuum the area around the cage and wipe down all of the nearby surfaces with a wet cloth.

It may be necessary to repeat this process several times to eradicate the mites completely. Accordingly, the very best strategy is to avoid contracting mites in the first place. This is why it is important to purchase your snake from a reliable breeder or retailer, and keep your snake quarantined from potential mite vectors.

As an example, even if you purchase your snake from a reliable source, provide excellent husbandry and clean the cage regularly, you can end up battling mites if your friend brings his snake – which has a few mites – to your house.

It may even be possible for mites to crawl onto your hands or clothes, hop off when you return home and make their way to your snake.

Make it a practice to inspect your snake and his cage regularly. Look in the crease under the snake's lower jaw, near the eyes and near the vent -- common places in which mites hide. It can also be helpful to wipe down your snake with a damp, white paper towel. After wiping down the snake, observe the towel to see if any mites are present.

Chemical treatments are also available to combat mites, but you must be very careful with such substances. Beginners should rely on their veterinarian to prescribe or suggest the appropriate products to use.

Avoid repurposing lice treatments or other chemicals, as is often encouraged by other hobbyists. Such non-intended use may be very dangerous, and it is often in violation of Federal laws.

New hobbyists should consult with their veterinarian if they suspect that their snake has mites. Mite eradication is often a challenging ordeal that your veterinarian can help make easier.

Long-Term Anorexia

While short-term fasts of a few weeks are common among snakes, those that last longer than this may be cause for concern. If your snake refuses food, ensure that its habitat is set up ideally with ample hiding opportunities and access to appropriate temperatures. If none of these factors requires attention, consult your veterinarian. Above all, do not panic – snakes can go very long periods of time without eating.

Your veterinarian will want to make sure that your snake is in good health, as respiratory infections, mouth rot or internal parasites may cause him to refuse food.

Some snakes refuse food in the winter or breeding season, as they would in the wild. While you should consult with your veterinarian the first time this happens, it shouldn't cause you much concern in subsequent years.

Healthy carpet pythons are alert and responsive to their surroundings.

Chapter 15: Breeding Carpet pythons

Breeding carpet pythons is a relatively straightforward process, and requires only a few basic steps to complete. However, keepers must consider the prospect of captive reproduction carefully at the outset.

Pre-Breeding Considerations

Before you set out to breed your carpet pythons, consider the decision carefully. Unfortunately, few keepers realize the implications of breeding their snakes before they set out to do so.

Ask yourself if you will be able to:

- Provide the proper care for the female while gravid
- Afford emergency veterinary services if necessary
- Be willing to remove the young from the same cage hosting an angry, protective female.
- Provide housing for 20 or more babies
- Provide food for 20 or more babies
- Dedicate the time to establishing 20 or more babies
- Find the time to care for 20 or more babies
- Find new homes for 20 or more babies
- Afford to heat up to 20 baby snake habitats

Few people are able to do all of these things. But unfortunately, they see the price tags associated with many snakes, and instantly envision themselves becoming snake breeders. However, the vast majority of people that try to breed snakes for profit fail.

Becoming a snake breeder means that, depending on the area in which you live, you may have to obtain licenses, insurance or permits to do so legally.

Sexing Carpet Pythons

Obviously, you must have at least one sexual pair of animals to hope for reproductive success. In fact, it is wise to verify the sex of *all* snakes slated for breeding programs, except those who have successfully reproduced in the past.

However, determining the sex of carpet pythons (and most other snakes) is somewhat difficult, as their genitals are completely internal and they exhibit very few obvious signs that indicate their sex.

Females also tend to have larger abdomens and total lengths than males of the same age, but these differences are often very subtle and subject to individual variation. Additionally, most males have larger spurs than females of the same size do.

Experienced keepers often attempt a technique called manual eversion, in which gentle pressure is applied to the base of a snake's tail. If performed correctly, the pressure will cause the vent to open and the hemipenes (if present) to evert. Those with hemipenes are considered male and those that fail to evert hemipenes are considered female.

However, manual eversion is not an ideal method for determining a snake's sex. Males eventually become strong enough to resist the pressure, which would cause them to be mistaken for females. Accordingly, it is only a suitable technique for very young individuals – it is of little use with mature animals.

A technique called "probing" is generally considered to be the best method for determining the sex of your snakes. Probing involves the insertion of a smooth, blunt steel probe into a snake's cloaca.

The idea is that if the snake is a male, the probe will pass deeply into his tail, as it travels through one of the two inverted hemipenes. If the snake is a female, the probe will end at the base of a short, wide pocket, and only penetrate a short distance.

However, the person performing the technique must interpret the results to some degree, so misidentifications occur from time to time.

Because the technique requires a strong understanding of your snake's internal anatomy and some finesse, it is best for beginners to seek out knowledgeable keepers or veterinarians for assistance. Additionally, as improper techniques may lead to injuries, beginners should never attempt to probe an animal without proper instruction.

Pre-Breeding Conditioning

Breeding reptiles always entails risk, so it is wise to refrain from breeding any animals that are not in excellent health. Breeding is especially stressful for female carpet pythons, who must carry the developing young for several months.

Animals slated for breeding trials must have excellent body weight, but obesity is to be avoided, as it is associated with reproductive problems. Ensure that the snakes are appropriately hydrated, and are free of parasites, infections and injuries.

Cycling

Cycling is the terms used to describe the climactic changes keepers impose upon their animals, which seek to mimic the natural seasonal changes in an animal's natural habitat.

For example, keepers may simulate winter conditions by reducing the enclosure temperatures and providing fewer hours of lighting. These changes are often necessary to stimulate captive reptiles into producing eggs, sperm or both.

However, because some carpet pythons hail from areas with relatively consistent annual temperatures and little fluctuation in photoperiod, cycling is not always necessary for successful reproduction. Nevertheless, most keepers provide a slight dip in temperatures for 1 to 2 months to help improve breeding success.

Successful breeders employ a wide variety of cycling regimens, but most involve a slight reduction in nighttime temperatures, and some also include a slight drop in daytime temperatures. Some keepers also allow the humidity levels to drop during the cycling period, or they manipulate the photoperiod to yield slightly longer nights and slightly shorter days.

For example, you may begin cycling your pythons in early November by allowing their habitat temperature to drop about 5 degrees Fahrenheit (about 2 to 3 degrees Celsius) and reduce the number daylight hours (and therefore the amount of hours that the basking spot is turned on) by one or two hours.

You would keep the temperatures in this range until the beginning of January, at which time you would restore the typical thermal environment, photoperiod and humidity levels. Some keepers actually increase the humidity immediately following cycling, to help simulate a rainy season.

However, because different carpet python subspecies hail from rather different climates, it is important to consider the subspecies in question before establishing a cycling protocol. Those from the southern end of the group's range likely require cooler temperatures to stimulate successful reproduction than those from the northern end of the group's range do.

Some pythons will begin refusing food with the onset of lower temperatures, while others will continue to feed.

Pairing

Once your carpet pythons have been cycled for 4 to 6 weeks, it is time to begin introducing the male to the female's enclosure.

Copulation may begin almost immediately, or it may take several hours to occur. The pair may copulate only once, or they may copulate several times over many days. It is usually wise to house the pair together for several days, to allow for multiple copulations, thereby helping to ensure good fertility.

Always take the time to separate the animals before feeding attempts to prevent accidents. However, many carpet pythons (particularly males) will refuse food until after the breeding season reaches its conclusion.

Eliciting Copulation

Occasionally, males fail to court and breed the female with whom they are paired. Sometimes, there is nothing that can be done to change this – some pairs are simply not compatible. However, python breeders have devised a number of techniques over the years that may help encourage copulation.

The presence of other males may incite the male's competitive instincts, and cause him to breed. While you can use another live male python to accomplish this, the two males may begin to engage in combat. You can instead try to place the shed skin of another male in the cage with the pair -- this is often effective and avoids putting the males at risk.

If you do not have another male or shed skin to use (or you have tried such techniques unsuccessfully), it may be helpful to scratch the male near his spurs, back and vent area. This is thought to simulate the feeling caused by another male's spurs, which may spark his competitive instincts.

Some python breeders have noticed that copulation often occurs during thunderstorms. While you cannot control the weather, you can certainly take advantage of storms when they occur. If possible, open the windows to lower the barometric pressure in the room. Misting the snakes with water may also encourage breeding activity.

If you have tried every method possible to elicit breeding activity, and had no success, separate the animals and wait for one of them to shed. Place the animals back together immediately after the shed and hope for the best.

Ultimately, some pairs are just incompatible. In such cases there is little the keeper can do except try to switch animals and hope for better chemistry with a new pair.

Care of the Gravid Female

With some luck, the female will ovulate shortly after the animals have bred. When this occurs, the unfertilized ova are released from the ovaries and moved into the oviducts, where they are fertilized by waiting sperm.

While not always seen by keepers, ovulation causes a large swelling in the female's abdomen, particularly if both ovaries ovulate simultaneously. In extreme cases, the size of the bulge can exceed that produced by a large food item. This is typically not a cause for concern – to the contrary, ovulation ensures that the female will eventually deposit eggs.

Ovulation typically lasts a matter of hours, but sometimes continues for 24 hours or more. After ovulation, the female can be considered gravid. Most females will shed their skin shortly after this occurs. This is referred to as the post-ovulation shed.

Remove the male from the female's enclosure once ovulation occurs or the female begins displaying such signs that she is gravid. This will help keep her stress level low and allow you to provide better care for her.

Do not handle gravid females unless absolutely necessary, and try to keep their stress level as low as possible. It is often wise to cover the female's enclosure to give her additional privacy.

Gravid females may alter their behavior in several subtle ways. They may bask for prolonged periods of time or become more reclusive. Some may adopt darker colors for the duration of the pregnancy. After initially exhibiting an increased appetite, most females cease feeding as parturition approaches.

Near the end of the gestation, females develop very plump abdomens. In some cases, they may lie on their sides or backs, in an effort to expose the developing embryos to overhead heat sources.

Most female carpet pythons deposit eggs about three to four weeks after their post-ovulation shed.

Egg Deposition

Female carpet pythons may deposit eggs at any hour of the day. If secluded in a private egg-deposition chamber, it may be necessary to check on her regularly, to avoid missing the event.

The eggs may be adhered to each other in a tight bundle when you find them, or they may be scattered. While some keepers separate stuck eggs, the task requires considerable skill; accordingly, novices should simply leave such eggs attached.

In both cases, it is necessary to keep the eggs oriented in the same way they were when you picked them up. Mark the tops of the eggs with a graphite pencil to keep them oriented the correct way.

Be aware that some females become extremely defensive after depositing eggs. It may help to place a soft towel over her body, which will allow you to scoop up her body while keeping her relatively calm.

Remove the young while the female is soaking and perform a thorough cage cleaning to remove any lingering odor of parturition – some females may be reluctant to feed if they can still smell the litter.

Maternal Incubation

If you decide to let your carpet python incubate her eggs, you should disturb her as little as possible. It is important to prevent the eggs from getting wet, but a high humidity should be maintained in the cage.

Check on the female and her clutch periodically, but try not to disturb her more than necessary. About 50 days into the process, you should begin checking the eggs more frequently. When they start to dent, hatching time is drawing near.

Be sure that the young will have some way to climb out of the egg chamber once they hatch. Once several of the young have hatched, you may want to consider removing the female.

Artificial Incubation

Most breeders elect to incubate their eggs artificially. If nothing else, doing so allows the female to begin feeding sooner than if you allow her to incubate the eggs herself.

However, removing the eggs from the female can be a difficult job.

Often, females become extremely defensive during this time – this includes females who are typically tame, trustworthy snakes. However, some females may remain docile despite attempts to remove the eggs.

Always have a helper when trying to remove a female from her eggs. Doing so makes the process easier on both the keeper and the kept.

Begin by trying to grasp the female gently behind the head. Immediately use your other hand to stabilize the egg mass. Have your helper use both hands to contain the eggs, and slowly remove your hand from the eggs. Then begin using your free hand to unwind the female.

With patience and a firm but gentle touch, you will successfully remove her from her eggs. In some cases, it may be easier to unwind her partially, and remove the eggs while she remains in her cage.

Egg Incubation

To incubate the eggs artificially, you will need some type of incubator. Beginners should purchase an entry-level, commercially produced product, but advanced keepers can construct their own.

Incubators need not be elaborate to produce good results, but they must be well insulated and maintain a very consistent internal temperature. Always use a separate thermometer as a backup to the incubator's thermometer.

Most often, the eggs are placed in small egg boxes, which are in turn placed in the incubator. Virtually any small plastic boxes will suffice for containing the eggs.

Some keepers place moistened vermiculite or perlite in the egg boxes as a substrate. Other keepers suspend the eggs directly over water. Both strategies can generate success, but vermiculite offers more room for error. Moisten the vermiculite just enough so that it clumps when squeezed in the hand.

Incubate carpet python eggs between 87 and 88 degrees Fahrenheit. The humidity should be as high as possible, without causing condensation to form on or over the eggs. Eggs do require fresh air, but a few very small (1/8th inch) holes suffice.

The eggs normally hatch in about 55 to 65 days. The young do not all emerge at once and the earliest hatchlings may emerge up to 48 hours or so before the last emerge.

Do not remove hatchlings from their eggs. Doing so may cause their umbilicus to tear, opening them to infection and cutting off a vital energy source. If any emerge and are still connected to the yolk, allow it to fall off on its own.

Neonatal Husbandry

Begin by removing all of the young who have broken free of their egg sack and absorbed their entire egg yolk. You can place these individuals in a small, communal "nursery" until they complete their first shed.

A small plastic storage box makes a good nursery. You will need to heat the nursery with a heating pad or heat lamp, to keep it around 80 degrees Fahrenheit (26 to 27 degrees Celsius) at all times.

Keep the nursery simple, with a damp, paper-towel substrate and crumpled paper for hiding. You must also provide a wide, shallow water dish for the young snakes. This will help increase the humidity, but because it is shallow, will not serve as a drowning hazard for the young.

Young that have not yet emerged from their egg sacs or absorbed their yolks should be handled very delicately. Place each such snake in a separate enclosure, set up just like the communal nursery.

Do not attempt to break open the egg sack or pull on the egg yolk – simply be patient and keep such snakes warm and humid until they emerge on their own.

As they shed, individual snakes should be moved to their own enclosure. Begin feeding trials soon after their first shed. Many pythons may refuse food the first or second attempt, so patience is required. By contrast, others will feed with little pause at the first opportunity.

Hatchling carpet pythons are often colored differently than the adults are.

Chapter 16: Further Reading

Never stop learning about your new pet's natural history, biology and captive care. This is the only way to ensure your pet's well-being and grow as a keeper.

Books

While brick and mortar bookstores are a viable place to search for books, online retailers dealers often offer more titles. Your local library may also carry some books about reptiles, snakes or carpet pythons, which you can borrow for no charge. University libraries also serve as valuable resources, and they are especially helpful for finding obscure or academically oriented materials.

Herpetology: An Introductory Biology of Amphibians and Reptiles
By Laurie J. Vitt, Janalee P. Caldwell
Top of Form
Bottom of Form
Academic Press, 2013

Understanding Reptile Parasites: A Basic Manual for Herpetoculturists & Veterinarians
By Roger Klingenberg D.V.M.
Advanced Vivarium Systems, 1997

Infectious Diseases and Pathology of Reptiles: Color Atlas and Text
Elliott Jacobson
CRC Press

Designer Reptiles and Amphibians
Richard D. Bartlett, Patricia Bartlett
Barron's Educational Series

What's Wrong with My Snake?
John Rossi, Roxanne Rossi
BowTie Press

Designer Reptiles and Amphibians
Richard D. Bartlett, Patricia Bartlett
Barron's Educational Series

Boas and Pythons of the World
Mark O'Shea
New Holland Publishers

Snakes: Everything about Selection, Care, Nutrition, Diseases, Breeding, and Behavior
Richard D. Bartlett, Patricia Pope Bartlett
Barron's Educational Series

Magazines

Because magazines are typically published monthly or bi-monthly, they can offer more up-to-date information than books can. Magazine articles are obviously not as comprehensive as books typically are, but they still have considerable value.

Reptiles Magazine
www.reptilesmagazine.com/
Covering reptiles commonly kept in captivity.

Practical Reptile Keeping
http://www.practicalreptilekeeping.co.uk/
Practical Reptile Keeping is a popular publication aimed at beginning and advanced hobbyists. Topics include the care and maintenance of popular reptiles as well as information on wild reptiles.

Websites

Anyone with a computer and internet connection can launch a website and say virtually anything they want about carpet pythons. Accordingly, as with all other research, consider the source of the information before making any husbandry decisions.

The Reptile Report
www.thereptilereport.com/
The Reptile Report is a news-aggregating website that accumulates interesting stories and features about reptiles from around the world.

Kingsnake.com
www.kingsnake.com
After starting as a small website for gray-banded kingsnake enthusiasts, Kingsnake.com has become one of the largest reptile-oriented portals in the hobby. The site features classified advertisements, a breeder directory, message forums and other resources.

The Vivarium and Aquarium News
www.vivariumnews.com/
The online version of the former print publication, The Vivarium and Aquarium News provides in-depth coverage of different reptiles and amphibians in a captive and wild context.

Journals

Journals are the primary place professional scientists turn when they need to learn about carpet pythons. While they may not make light reading, hobbyists stand to learn a great deal from peer-reviewed journals.

Herpetologica
www.hljournals.org/

Published by The Herpetologists' League, Herpetologica, and its companion publication, Herpetological Monographs cover all aspects of reptile and amphibian research.

Journal of Herpetology
www.ssarherps.org/
Produced by the Society for the Study of Reptiles and Amphibians, the Journal of Herpetology is a peer-reviewed publication covering a variety of reptile-related topics.

Copeia
www.asihcopeiaonline.org/
Copeia is published by the American Society of Ichthyologists and Herpetologists. A peer-reviewed journal, Copeia covers all aspects of the biology of reptiles, amphibians and fish.

Nature
www.nature.com/
Although Nature covers all aspects of the natural world, many issues contain information that snake enthusiasts are sure to find interesting.

Supplies

You can obtain most of what you need to maintain carpet pythons through a combination of local home improvement and pet stores, but online retailers offer another option.

Big Apple Pet Supply
http://www.bigappleherp.com
Big Apple Pet Supply carries common husbandry equipment, including lamps, water dishes and substrates.

LLLReptile
http://www.lllreptile.com
LLL Reptile carries a wide variety of husbandry tools, heating devices, lighting products and more.

Doctors Foster and Smith
http://www.drsfostersmith.com
Foster and Smith is a veterinarian-owned retailer that supplies husbandry-related items to pet keepers.

Support Organizations
Sometimes, the best way to learn about carpet pythons is to reach out to other keepers and breeders. Check out these organizations, and search for others in your geographic area.

The National Reptile & Amphibian Advisory Council
http://www.nraac.org/
The National Reptile & Amphibian Advisory Council seeks to educate the hobbyists, legislators and the public about reptile and amphibian related issues.

American Veterinary Medical Association
www.avma.org
The AVMA is a good place for Americans to turn if you are having trouble finding a suitable reptile veterinarian.

The World Veterinary Association
http://www.worldvet.org/
The World Veterinary Association is a good resource for finding suitable reptile veterinarians worldwide.

References

Abigail S. Tucker a, G. J. (2014). Evolution and developmental diversity of tooth regeneration. *Seminars in Cell & Developmental Biology*.

Anderson, S. P. (2003). The Phylogenetic Definition of Reptilia. *Systematic Biology*.

Christian, G. S. (1998). Standard metabolic rate and preferred body temperatures in some Australian pythons. *Australian Journal of Zoology*.

D. Pearson, R. S. (2002). Geographic Variation in Sexual Size Dimorphism within a Single Snake Species. *Oecologia* .

D. Person, R. S. (2002). Sex-specific Niche Partitioning and Sexual Size Dimorphism in Australian Pythons. *Biological Journal of the Linnean Society*.

F. BRISCHOUX, L. P. (2010). Insights into the adaptive significance of vertical pupil shape in snakes. *Journal of Evolutionary Biology*.

Fitzgerald, R. S. (1995). Variation in mating systems and sexual size dimorphism between populations of the Australian python Morelia spilota . *Oecologia*.

Fitzgerald, R. S. (1996). Large Snakes in a Mosaic Rural Landscape: The Ecology of Carpet Pythons Morelia spilota (Serpentes: Pythonidae) in Coastal Eastern Australia. *Biological Conservation*.

G. W. Heard, D. B. (2004). Habitat use by the inland carpet python (Morelia spilota metcalfei: Pythonidae): Seasonal relationships with habitat structure and prey distribution in a rural landscape. *Austral Ecology*.

Heard, G., Robertson, P., Black, D., Barrow, G., Johnson, P., Hurley, V., & Allen, G. (2006). Canid Predation: A Potentially

Significant Threat to Relic Populations of the Inland Carpet Python 'Morelia Spilota Metcalfei' (Pythonidae) in Victoria. *The Victorian Naturalist*.

Lígia Pizzatto, S. M.-S. (2007). Life-history adaptations to arboreality in snakes. . *Ecology*.

Lyons, D. J. (2011). Distribution, ecological attributes and trade of the New Guinea carpet python (Morelia spilota) in Indonesia. *Australian Journal of Zoology*.

O'Shea, M. (1996). *A guide to the Snakes of Papua New Guinea*. Beaumont Publishing.

O'Shea, M. (2007). *Boas and Pythons of the World*. New Holland Publishers.

Proske, J. W. (1968). Infrared Receptors in the Facial Pits of the Australian Python Morelia spilotes. *Science* .

S. Fearn, B. R. (2002). Pythons in the pergola: the ecology of 'nuisance' carpet pythons (Morelia spilota) from suburban habitats in south-eastern Queensland. *Wildlife Research*.

Shine, D. Y. (1997). Thermal influences on foraging ability: body size, posture and cooling rate of an ambush predator, the python Morelia spilota. *Functional Ecology*.

Index

Achilles tendonitis, 124
Anorexia, 105
Aquariums, 43
Aspen, 64
Bleach, 76
Breeding, 77
cage, 35, 42, 43, 44, 45, 46, 52, 53, 54, 60, 100, 101, 103, 104
Cleaning, 73, 74
Copulation, 110
Cork Bark, 67
Cypress Mulch, 63
Dimensions, 42
Feeding, 77, 83
Gender, 38, 78
Heat, 32, 50, 51, 52, 53, 54
Heat Cables, 53
Heat Pads, 52
Heat Tape, 53
Heating, 54
Homemade Cages, 45
Hot Rocks, 54
Humid Hides, 68
husbandry, 118, 119, 120
Husbandry, 114

Lights, 57, 60
mites, 44, 102, 103, 104, 105
Mouth rot, 100
Newspaper, 67
Orchid Bark, 64
Paper Towels, 67
plastic storage boxes, 45
Prey, 80, 81
probe, 48, 56, 57
Regurgitation, 83
Rheostats, 55
Screen Cages, 46
Substrate, 63
Temperature, 47
Temperatures, 47
Thermal Gradients, 48
Thermal Mass, 58
Thermometers, 47
Thermostats, 56, 57
veterinarian, 34, 41, 47, 74, 76, 96, 97, 98, 99, 100, 101, 102, 104, 105, 120
veterinarian's, 47
Water, 32, 89

Published by IMB Publishing 2016

Copyright and Trademarks: This publication is Copyrighted 2016 by IMB Publishing. All products, publications, software and services mentioned and recommended in this publication are protected by trademarks. In such instance, all trademarks & copyright belong to the respective owners. All rights reserved. No part of this book may be reproduced or transferred in any form or by any means, graphic, electronic, or mechanical, including photocopying, recording, taping, or by any information storage retrieval system, without the written permission of the authors. Pictures used in this book are either royalty free pictures bought from stock-photo websites or have the source mentioned underneath the picture.

Disclaimer and Legal Notice: This product is not legal or medical advice and should not be interpreted in that manner. You need to do your own due-diligence to determine if the content of this product is right for you. The author and the affiliates of this product are not liable for any damages or losses associated with the content in this product. While every attempt has been made to verify the information shared in this publication, neither the author nor the affiliates assume any responsibility for errors, omissions or contrary interpretation of the subject matter herein. Any perceived slights to any specific person(s) or organization(s) are purely unintentional. We have no control over the nature, content and availability of the web sites listed in this book. The inclusion of any web site links does not necessarily imply a recommendation or endorse the views expressed within them. IMB Publishing takes no responsibility for, and will not be liable for, the websites being temporarily unavailable or being removed from the Internet. The accuracy and completeness of information provided herein and opinions stated herein are not guaranteed or warranted to produce any particular results, and the advice and strategies, contained herein may not be suitable for every individual. The author shall not be liable for any loss incurred as a consequence of the use and application, directly or indirectly, of any information presented in this work. This publication is designed to provide information in regards to the subject matter covered. The information included in this book has been compiled to give an overview of the subject s and detail some of the symptoms, treatments etc. that are available to people with this condition. It is not intended to give medical advice. For a firm diagnosis of your condition, and for a treatment plan suitable for you, you should consult your doctor or consultant. The writer of this book and the publisher are not responsible for any damages or negative consequences following any of the treatments or methods highlighted in this book. Website links are for informational purposes and should not be seen as a personal endorsement; the same applies to the products detailed in this book. The reader should also be aware that although the web links included were correct at the time of writing, they may become out of date in the future.

www.ingramcontent.com/pod-product-compliance
Lightning Source LLC
LaVergne TN
LVHW021714080426
835510LV00010B/991